Welcome to Your
CRISIS

Also by Laura Day

THE CIRCLE

PRACTICAL INTUITION IN LOVE

PRACTICAL INTUITION FOR SUCCESS

PRACTICAL INTUITION

Welcome to Your
CRISIS

HOW TO USE THE POWER

OF CRISIS TO CREATE

THE LIFE YOU WANT

LAURA DAY

LITTLE, BROWN AND COMPANY
NEW YORK • BOSTON

Little, Brown and Company
Time Warner Book Group
1271 Avenue of the Americas, New York, NY 10020
Visit our Web site at www.twbookmark.com

First Edition: May 2006

Library of Congress Cataloging-in-Publication Data
Day, Laura.
Welcome to your crisis : how to use the power of crisis to create the
life you want / Laura Day — 1st ed.
    p. cm.
  ISBN-10: 0-316-11464-2 (hardcover)
  ISBN-13: 978-0-316-11464-6 (hardcover)
  1. Self-actualization (Psychology) 2. Life change events —
Psychological aspects. I. Title.
BF637 .S4D392 2006
155.9'3 — DC22   2005024397

10   9   8   7   6   5   4   3   2   1

Q-MART

Book design by Meryl Sussman Levavi

Printed in the United States of America

I DEDICATE THIS BOOK TO MY DEAR FRIEND AND THE GODFATHER OF MY SON SAMSON, KEVIN HUVANE. THANK YOU FOR YOUR VISION. THANK YOU FOR YOUR FAITH. AND THANK YOU FOR ALWAYS HAVING A SOLUTION AT THREE O'CLOCK IN THE MORNING (PACIFIC STANDARD TIME). RALPH WALDO EMERSON SAID THAT EVERY WALL IS A DOOR. THANK YOU FOR PROVING HIM RIGHT!

CONTENTS

PREFACE

Welcome to your crisis?

The idea that a crisis might have some positive aspects probably sounds unfeeling. Crises are painful, difficult, and threatening situations, to be sure. I wouldn't wish a crisis on anyone.

Unfortunately, crises are inevitable features of our lives. Learning how to navigate crises well, then, is a crucial life skill. And since not all crises can be avoided, why not meet them head on and embrace them? As you'll discover shortly, crises force us to make long-overdue changes in our lives and can serve as catalysts for remarkable positive transformations.

If we allow them to.

The insights and recommendations in this book are based on my own observations and experiences in helping people and organizations handle crises. Some key elements in my methodology are corroborated by the work of others, such as Hans Selye in the field of stress (Selye observed that positive events can induce just as much stress as do many negative ones), Mihaly Csikszentmihalyi in the field of optimal human functioning (who observed that we feel most alive when our abilities are fully engaged by challenges), and sociologist Charles Fritz in the field of human behavior during disasters.

Fritz's seminal observations about disasters offer compelling insights into how you and I should handle our personal crises. If a crisis is bad, a disaster must be that much worse. Yet as Fritz pointed out, disasters reveal positive truths about human behavior. As in crises, disasters elicit many of our best qualities as human and social beings. So can our crises.

Disasters have been in the news this past year, most

poignantly in the instance of the devastation wreaked on New Orleans by Hurricane Katrina. Closer to my home, I have witnessed other disasters in my own neighborhood. I live in New York City, mere blocks from the site of the former World Trade Center.

So I speak from firsthand experience when I point out — as I'm sure you have experienced in any disasters you've witnessed up close — that far from leading to chaos or worse, disasters often bring out the best in people. We've all seen news coverage of looting and other acts of predatory opportunism that occur during disasters. While such acts may make for riveting journalism, they are by far the exception rather than the norm. In disasters most people act with compassion, selflessly and tirelessly working together to help others afflicted by the disaster.

The key aspect of a disaster that minimizes its harm, as it inspires and ennobles everyday people, is that the experience is *shared*. The impact of Hurricane Katrina was so horrific precisely because the flood itself prevented people from acting *as* a community and from sharing the disaster's emotional, psychological, physical, and other burdens.

Crises and disasters sound awful, and indeed they are.

Our daily lives, by contrast, seem prosaic if not idyllic. If we are honest with ourselves, however, a closer look at our lives reveals a different reality. Our routine, everyday lives are filled with conflicts, stresses, and frustrations. Even when we are not beset by petty concerns and obligations, our lives rarely demand our full engagement; much of the time we are simply going through the motions. And apart from our families and close friends, and to a lesser degree our neighbors, we live in an atomized, fragmented society, having little interaction with those around us. The key point here is we keep our everyday crises, in sharp distinction with the shared experience of public disasters, well hidden from others, sometimes even from our closest friends and loved ones.

What lessons can we learn from the inspiring heroism and effectiveness of individuals during disasters that we can apply to our handling of the crises in our personal lives? Let's examine the characteristics of disasters to see how they overlap with or differ from the characteristics of our personal crises.

A disaster dwarfs everything else in the lives of those affected. A disaster simplifies and streamlines our lives. In a disaster, the most pressing needs are concrete and relegate all other needs to the background as minor distractions to the real work that must get done. Notice that in a disaster, few people are as bad off as are the worst affected. Everyone focuses on the plight of those worse off, and the entire community is galvanized to participate in relief efforts.

A "we're-all-in-this-together" attitude prevails, and a new community — those affected by the disaster — arises to address the most urgent needs. Everyone pitches in to help and is given a sense of mission, a larger purpose outside themselves, and the resulting tight-knit social solidarity of the disaster community is astonishing.

Because the disaster was caused by something external, individuals do not blame themselves or others for their misfortune, nor does anyone feel guilt or shame. Everyone feels free to open up and communicate with others in the disaster community, providing mutual physical and emotional support. Mourning and grieving for the disaster's losses, suffering, and privations are intense, but shared by many.

Two of the key features of disaster relief, then, are the

importance of sharing as much as possible, and of taking care of business. Contrast this effective functioning in the face of public disaster with the ineffective handling with which most of us grapple with our private crises. Most of us tend to keep our crises to ourselves, often out of shame. We allow the crisis to overwhelm our ability to get on with our mundane, day-to-day obligations.

I come from a family of doctors and have been an intuitive healer for my entire adult life. In the field of medicine, the word *crisis* has a specific meaning: that sudden point in the course of a disease when the disease either gets dramatically worse or turns around and gets dramatically better. Our everyday crises present us with similar junctions, at which our lives can turn dramatically worse or dramatically better depending on the actions we take. I wrote this book to help you make sure your path out of crisis is both positive and enriching.

Welcome to Your
CRISIS

INTRODUCTION

Many people who pick up this book sense that they need a big change — either in themselves or in their lives. Even readers who feel that everything is going great in their lives still feel that something is not working, that something is missing.

ॐ

Who in normal circumstances consults an intuitive healer? Consulting an intuitive is not like going to a physician for a physical checkup. *People seek my advice because their lives are in crisis.*

Guiding people through their crises is not what I do — *it is who I am.* I've been this person since childhood, when I found myself thrust into the role of helping my mother through her crises.

Ever since then I've been a beacon for people in crisis. I use my intuitive skills to help these people find new lives — and new selves. I also help them develop their intuitive abilities so they, too, can draw on the wisdom of others.

·⁂·

My first book, *Practical Intuition,* outlines a process that anyone can use to gather important information through the intuitive sense. My last book, *The Circle: How the Power of a Single Wish Can Change Your Life,* reveals the master formula for conscious creation: how you can realize any goal through the focused use of intuition, intellect, and behavior.

This book — and you needn't have read any of my others to utilize this one — will give you a reliable map through any loss or life change you may experience. You will learn a way of self-growth, a way of creating your life passionately and effectively.

≥о

Welcome to Your Crisis is about helping you master changes in your life, both the changes you want to make and the changes thrust upon you. This book can guide you through the journey that is your life. I will reveal the challenges you'll face at each stage and show you how to navigate successfully through the many life cycles that you will experience.

≥о

This book is a practical one, designed to help you create positive change in your life. To get the most value from this book, you'll need to complete its exercises conscientiously. I recommend that you start a journal to take notes and to keep all your work in one place; many exercises build on earlier ones, so you should keep all your "self-work" handy.

The exercises in this book, even the briefest ones, allow you to repattern or reprogram your thinking, feeling, and choosing. Perform them regularly and casually, as an organic part of your everyday routines. Ultimately these exercises will become programmed into your subconscious, and you will be able to rely on them when you fall back into old, sometimes self-destructive responses. You are giving yourself new choices in your journey to create a new life.

⋇

I'm not asking you to accept everything in this book on faith. If you're going through a crisis, your skepticism may be in high gear.

That's okay. All I ask is that you approach the concepts and complete the exercises with an open mind. You don't even have to believe anything I say.

The Danish physicist Niels Bohr, one of the titans of twentieth-century science, was greeting a journalist at his rustic home in the countryside. Nailed above the door of his house was a horseshoe, a folk talisman to attract good luck.

The journalist, puzzled at this evidence of superstition on the threshold of the great scientist's house, remarked, "Dr. Bohr, I'm surprised to see that you believe in the magical power of horseshoes." "Oh, no," Bohr replied, "I don't believe in horseshoes. But I understand that they work whether or not you believe in them."

The laws of the universe are like that: they don't require your belief in them to work. Gravity pulls everyone down with or without our awareness, much less belief. Similarly, the path outlined in this book is in harmony with the laws of the universe, and it will work for you as it has worked for countless others in crisis over the past twenty years — as it has worked for me.

჻

I've been there.

When I was thirty-three years old, I gave birth to my son — and my marriage ended. I remember the moment I realized that my divorce was not going to be a simple affair. The checks stopped coming from my husband, and I didn't have a place to live.

My husband's family, whom I had considered my family since I was sixteen, not only ceased speaking to me but also became active adversaries to my survival. My lawyer, my accountant, and my investment advisors all became part of his camp because that's where the money was. All I had was my baby and the few friends that remained.

When I was married, all my financial needs were taken care of, so I didn't need to work. After my separation I had nothing — less than nothing, since I had a costly legal battle ahead of me. I went from never having had to make a living or even to deal with the world in any practical way to having to support myself and a baby. I had never earned more than fifteen thousand dollars in a year, and those earnings were a by-product of the pro bono work I did in the field of intuition and healing.

For the first year of my son's life, he and I slept on a futon on the living-room floor of a friend's apartment. I had met my husband at sixteen; I had no concept of who I was in the world without him. My beautiful, miraculous baby was my saving grace. The delight I had with my son considerably lessened the terror and confusion of my new circumstances.

When it was clear that my husband and I would divorce, he fought me for custody of the son I'd raised on my own since his birth. By this time I had nearly exhausted my savings, and my lawyer informed me that fighting a court battle could cost a million dollars, possibly more. My husband had his enormous trust fund; money was no problem for him. A million dollars to keep my son — it was like being told it would cost a million dollars to keep my heart beating!

Almost all the things that I believed about life and held dear — the people around me, my family, my love, my sense of self — were destroyed. Friends who'd known me as a free spirit, a wealthy wife, and a successful intuitive and healer looked at me now with compassion, if not pity. Many of the cherished qualities that defined me — my superb intuition, my ability to heal others, my trusting naïveté — were used against me in court in an effort to establish me as an unfit mother. I myself thought, "If I am so intuitive, how did I get myself into this mess?" (For answers to that question, see the chapter on inner roadblocks in my book *The Circle.*)

I was so unsure of myself and everything around me that when the other side accused me of being crazy, I actually went to a psychologist to have testing just in case their accusation was true, assuming that if I were truly crazy I would be the last to know it. I no longer knew who I was — or who I was no longer existed.

My old world and my trusted resources no longer existed, either. My own self — stripped out of context — seemed alien to me. I became prey to every piece of advice, every unscrupulous professional; I fell into every trap laid

out for me. I was terrified to take action, yet terrified to remain immobilized. I had a child to defend, so giving up
was not an option — but I was completely unequipped to
fight. I lost so much weight that people who didn't know
my circumstances thought that I was seriously ill. I had entered the Divorce Game, and apparently I was the only
player who didn't know the rules.

Every morning I would awaken and sit by the living-
room window, trying desperately to find a solution. One
morning I did the two things I was still capable of doing:
predicting future events (except, of course, for myself) and
writing (which I loved to do). I sat at my computer and
wrote down the ideas and memories that came to me. By the
time my son awakened, I had written eight pages about the
intuitive experiments I had done with a group of scientists.

When my son took his morning nap, I called a financial fund manager I knew. Boldly, I told him what the mar-
ket would do that day and asked him for a job. At the end
of that day, he gave me a job predicting the financial mar-
kets. I could do it by phone, half an hour a day, and in return, I received a salary and health insurance.

A few days later I took the pages I was writing to a

playdate. I wanted to work on them as Samson played with his friend and tried to eat sand. Another mother asked to see what I was working on. I showed her the pages. She said, "You have a book here."

I took the compliment graciously and thought no more of it until she handed me her card. She was a top New York book agent. Once the ball began rolling, it quickly picked up speed. That year I made enough to cover my expenses and enroll my son in a private nursery school. Within a few years I had earned nearly four million dollars — much of it was spent on the never-ending court battle. I fought and won custody of my son, found my voice in the world, fell in love with a fellow writer, wrote new books, bought back my apartment from my husband, and became part of a community that I love and admire.

The old "I" no longer existed, nor did the world in which she had lived. I had no new skills or sense of the world to take its place. Perhaps you, too, have been in similar straits, possibly more than once. I was given the gift of having something to offer in the world. All of this from the single darkest moment, when I thought I would lose my precious son.

My transformation was not achieved by magic. I learned the lessons in this book the hard way. It will be easier for you. I've been there. I will show you the way.

ஃ

You have the power to create positive, lasting change in your life. You are deciding right now, in this moment, what your future will be. Your continually deciding your own fate may seem like a frightening responsibility, but if you screw up this moment and get it wrong, you can decide again who you want to be in the *next* moment. It's all up to you.

If you are in crisis, you may have trouble accepting your power to change your situation. Even if you feel your life is all over, allow me at least to lead you step-by-step to a better future, one in which you'll be happy.

My goal is to make you aware of the dynamics of crisis and to support the process and make it tolerable. We cannot stop losses in our lives, but conscious living allows us to use any crisis in positive, transformative ways.

ஃ

Crisis is the challenge and the opportunity to uncover what we value, rediscover what we need, redefine what gives us pleasure, re-create a meaningful life, and reconfigure the inner workings of self. Crisis forces us to reach deep within ourselves, where we can discover treasured, powerful, *forgotten* parts of us that we hid long ago, even from *ourselves.* The lives we can create once we open this treasure chest of being exceed not only our expectations but also our imagination.

I know that it may be hard for you to believe, but your current crisis could be the best thing that ever happened to you. In fact you can make *sure* your crisis is the best thing that ever happened to you, even if it seems right now as if all is lost. You may feel that you made mistakes that you now hate yourself for, that you ruined everything good in your life, that everything you loved or needed is gone.

I have been there. Most people have. Right now you have the perfect opportunity to discover what you need to create a life beyond anything you could have previously imagined. A treasure chest of talents, desires, and personality traits — one you've kept locked away from the world, even from yourself, since you were too young to remember — exists for you to open now as an adult. Through this process of moving through crisis, you'll find yourself and the key to the most wonderful life that you can have. Crisis forces you to break down barriers and to entertain new possibilities, possibilities that may feel strange, yet are older and more authentic than anything that you are living to date.

We'll explore these matters later. For now simply notice which of your thoughts, feelings, dreams, responses, or ways of being surprise you. Simply notice, without judgment. Getting angry for the first time in your life may be the first step to real passion and creativity. Feeling depressed, if it is an unusual state for you, may be your doorway to knowing your true needs and feelings and to creating a fulfilling life.

- Have you had any unusual feelings lately?
- Have you been behaving or reacting differently of late?
- Have you noticed anything new, either in yourself or in others?

- When you notice people around you, where is your attention drawn? Whom do you envy?

Ask yourself these questions as you move through your day. Your current job is to make *you* more interesting to yourself than your crisis is! Become acquainted with yourself — your new self — as you would get to know a new friend. Be curious. Assume nothing. You are about to embark on a glorious, magnificent new chapter of your life — not *despite* your current crisis, but *because* of it!

Who Are You?

A Recurring Question to Contemplate

*W*ho are you? That simple question is far more profound than a first glance might suggest. Many people describe themselves in terms of their career (lawyer, carpenter, lab technician, NASCAR driver) or in terms of their relationships (wife, mother, best friend).

You are about to discover that how you define yourself

largely determines not only how the world perceives you, but also how effective you are in that world.

Which brings us to your first exercise.

Exercise: Who Are You?

Without giving you any particular expectations, I'd like you to answer each of the following questions with one sentence: *Who are you? Who were you before your last crisis? Who do you fear you are? Who do you wish you were?*

You'll want to refer to your answers in the coming days, weeks, and even years, so use the journal you've devoted to the exercises in this book.

Discussion

As I mentioned, there are countless ways to approach the task of describing yourself. Here are two examples:

> I am someone healing from knee surgery. I used to be a professional dancer. I guess now I'm someone who will never dance again. I wish I were healthy and able to dance.

I am an entrepreneur. I started a catering business when I lost my job in sales. I enjoy what I do, though sometimes the hours are brutal. I don't have as much free time as I used to; I suppose that's the trade-off for career autonomy.

Notice how you describe and define yourself. You are not, however, your self-description. You are not who you were. You are not your fears. You are not your wishes. You are a web of interdependent facts and feelings. If you confront these facts and feelings realistically and systematically, you will become someone you admire and your life will become something you treasure.

Your self-descriptions will change in the coming days, as you work through these chapters.

How You Define Yourself
Determines Your Vulnerability

How we define ourselves determines, then, how vulnerable — or how resilient — we are to life's changing fortunes. The wrenching changes that we experience in our lives are often painful because we identify so completely with how we describe ourselves. We identify with how we are defined by the structures around us: by our jobs, our relationships, our families, our successes. If we are fortunate we gain a better sense of our connection to others and to the world around us as we get older, and we begin the process of integrating ego into something that extends infinitely beyond it.

This concept is important because the crises in your life attack the very core of your sense of self. It is easy to understand how a person who identified herself, say, as a wife would feel that her life were over when her marriage ended. A successful young entrepreneur loses her company. Who is she now?

Transforming your sense of self enables you to rise above life's challenges — indeed, doing so enables you to use these same challenges to enrich your self-worth and your potential in life to enjoy, create, and achieve.

☙

As long as you cling to a narrow definition of yourself, you are vulnerable to any number of crises. Your self-concept is especially elusive when you are experiencing a major life change: you are no longer who you were, but you are not yet who you are becoming.

The importance of knowing who you are applies not just to individuals but also to groups, organizations, and companies. A company will begin its life providing one product or service, but when the world changes, the company's belief about what is important — the company's sense of self and identity — has to change as well. How ironic that Steven Jobs, the man who cofounded Apple as a computer company — only to be forced out — would return to lead Apple's rebirth as one of the world's premier consumer electronics companies.

You Are an Ecosystem

You will find it helpful to think of yourself not as an isolated being but as a vast ecosystem.

Consider a natural ecosystem and its enormous web of interconnected parts. The myriad parts of any ecosystem are intimately interrelated, woven into a complex, yet fragile, system.

That system is in dynamic balance; any minor fluctuations are easily absorbed by the system. Sometimes something from outside the ecosystem alters it dramatically. A new predator species arrives. A persistent drought exhausts the ecosystem's water supply.

Such disruptions are not readily absorbed but rather reverberate throughout the entire ecosystem. One species dies out, threatening the survival of another species that had depended on the first. A third species, previously preyed upon by the first, multiplies wildly. And so on.

Eventually balance will reestablish itself, of course, but the ecosystem will never be the same.

A tiny shift in perception or behavior can create monumental changes in the internal dynamics that you call your life.

We have all had the experience of being in a darkened theater when an exit door unexpectedly opens, flooding the darkness with light and transforming our perception of our surroundings and our place within those surroundings. We often live our lives avoiding those rays of light for fear of what they will illuminate, sometimes through small shifts in our growth or behavior and often through the imposition of others or of outside events. When that happens we must adjust to a new ecosystem and our new position within it.

Outer Changes Require and Reflect Inner Changes

Change is also difficult because we often attribute it to bad luck, to unconscious personal shortcomings, or to external forces beyond our knowledge or control. In other words we often refuse to take any responsibility for the major changes and upheavals that occur in our lives.

Some changes are beyond our direct control, such as a random act of violence or a random act of nature. Our *response* to any change, however, *is* within our control. Our response to a change is a powerful agent in how that change plays itself out in our lives.

❧

Why do resolutions fail? On New Year's Eve, people across the world prepare to start their lives afresh. A new year; a new life. They prepare their New Year's resolutions with great optimism and anticipation, welcoming in another new year with a list of challenges that they have failed at repeatedly in the past.

The next morning they awaken with the commitment that they will break a lifetime of habits in one day. They will lose ten pounds. Become successful. Find true love. Improve their marriages. Stop procrastinating. Get their tempers under control. Spend more time with their children. Making resolutions is comforting; all is well with the world.

The only problem, as we secretly know, is that this approach to behavior modification does not work. Indeed, setting ourselves overwhelming tasks is a formula for failure and self-hatred. We form our habits and behaviors over a lifetime. We become passionately attached to even the most unfulfilling ways of being merely because they are familiar. What makes us think, despite all our experiences to the contrary, that merely resolving to change leads to enduring change?

꙰

Many people find achieving lasting change difficult because they focus on the wrong "side of the equation." Something as practical as losing weight, for example, is not simply a physical change, but rather an outward reflection of an inner change your *self* has undergone. Most weight-loss plans fail because the person involved views the change — weight loss — as the process itself rather than the *result* of a process. The process of any lasting weight loss occurs when we *become* a person who does not need to overeat, a person who seeks to be active rather than sedentary, a person who fills her needs in ways other than through eating.

Losing weight, then, is merely the product of changing your *self.* Take a moment to grasp fully the importance of this truth. Outer changes reflect inner changes. To achieve in the world whatever you want — whether it is losing weight or gaining a promotion — focus on the inner changes you need to make, and the outer changes will follow naturally and inevitably.

Your every experience programs your response to future experiences, until you choose the experiences in the world that confirm a particular belief system. One way to define yourself, then, is in terms of your beliefs.

Sometimes you misjudge the world, and your core beliefs are challenged, if not shattered. A man you thought was
going to be with you forever moves to another city. Your
company eliminates your position. You experience a car ac-
cident. Sometimes you encounter a major, *unexpected* change.

Notice that when your reality challenges your beliefs,
and confronts you with the possibility that you will give
up those beliefs, you feel betrayed. All loss creates a sense
of betrayal.

When loss or other upheaval ruptures your beliefs,
you no longer exist in the same way — but you are provided with the possibility of a new beginning.

Regarding the world around us, our beliefs can act as spot-
lights, but they can also act as blinders. Our beliefs hide
any fact that threatens them and highlight any fact that
justifies or reinforces them. Our belief systems, that
is, excel at self-defense! We all have our blind spots —
especially about anything that challenges who we think we
are and what we've based our lives on.

Crisis occurs because our beliefs are so challenged that

they no longer have these boundaries in place. We are thrown into a search for new beliefs on which to pattern our actions and base our lives.

The great spiritual leaders throughout history had their beliefs so challenged that their entire beings were transformed. In allowing themselves to be transformed, they created brilliant examples for others to follow.

One of the joys of raising children is experiencing how their intellects grow not in small steps but in large leaps. At four, my son believed that his mother had all the answers. Mommy was truth. Then one day — truly one particular day; I remember it vividly — he realized that Mommy didn't have all of the answers. On this day his wisdom began. Now, as a teenager, he thinks he has all the answers. But as he grows into an adult, this phase of unshakable certitude will change, too. ("No it won't," he says. "Yes it will," I reply, patiently yet firmly. "You don't know anything," he counters. I bide my time.)

You are who you believe you are. You live in the world you believe you live in. Your beliefs frame and support everything you see in the world as well as your impulses and motivations. When you can no longer verify that reality, when your beliefs or your conditions no longer allow you to function effectively — you experience crisis.

I was thirty-five years old when my husband and I began our divorce. My son was two. Although my husband and I had been separated since my pregnancy, divorce litigation was a frightening new world.

When I was going through my divorce, I met a group of women in the courtroom halls where we spent our days in the costly and barbaric process of a divorce trial. To ensure that we retained custody of our children, we had to prove to a stranger — the judge — that we were viable human beings without our husbands, even if we personally had our doubts. We had to appear self-sufficient, remaining solid and unshaken in the face of accusations that even tabloids would be reluctant to print.

In reality we were all so beaten down by the demands of being single parents, of enduring the soul-crushing court processes, of paying our lawyers, and of being on the short end of the paycheck that we did not believe we amounted to much at all. Our formerly secure, sometimes even affluent, lives had been ruptured beyond repair. We were living in the garbage dump of our former lives.

At some point in the interminable divorce process, however, something "clicked" in all of us — a palpable, visceral change. Ironically, we had become so used to *faking* courage and self-sufficiency that we began to believe in and embody those traits! As our beliefs changed, we had the courage to call employers for jobs, to manage our lawyers differently, and to try to use our talents to succeed. As our beliefs about ourselves changed, we were able to capitalize on the opportunities around us.

I am still amazed that our personal transformations happened to us as a group, almost simultaneously. Nobody could look at any of us today and imagine us as the fragile, frightened, dependent women we had been not so long ago, waiting for our cases to be heard.

ॐ

In moments when we are required to adapt to change, our treasured internal responses and patterns — which supported us to this point — can become the barrier between us and success. New Year's resolutions fail because we make a list of changes we require of ourselves without addressing the many interconnected parts of the ecosystem in which they exist. People who need to lose weight or find better jobs or improve their relationships need to change something in their ecosystem — their patterns, surroundings, perceptions, or relationships — from which the goal is a natural and sustainable result.

When your beliefs change but your life does not change with them, you end up living a shadow life, striving to maintain your beliefs in a life and world you no longer inhabit. Consider Karen's story.

Karen was an advertising genius. She could find a way to package dirt and make you want to buy it. People around her always complimented her work, but she was clear she cared nothing about her work or her considerable talent. All she wanted to do was to marry, raise a family, and have someone take care of her. These needs meant everything to her.

Unfortunately, her relationships were a disaster. She always picked inappropriate or unavailable men. From month to month she was either euphoric about falling in love or devastated about having lost it. Many less-talented people received the promotions and the projects that would have displayed her gifts. Many less-lovely women married and had families. A single, anxious, thirty-nine-year-old, Karen was not fulfilling her potential either in work or in love. By putting her gifts at the "nothing end" of the spectrum and her domestic fantasy at the "everything end," she had disempowered herself to realize either potential.

 Everything in your life should have importance; nothing should be worthless.

To Change Your World, Change Yourself

Einstein's principle of relativity revolutionized how scientists view the universe and ultimately led to the discovery of atomic power. But the principle of relativity is more than a tool for scientists: it is a powerful *thinking* tool we can all use. This perspective will revolutionize how you view yourself and will give you untold power to shape your universe.

You are not a single, unrelated speck of energy. You create a field of energy, relationships, and outcomes. If your world changes, you change. The relativity principle tells us that this dynamic works the other way, too: *if you change yourself, your world changes — the universe changes.*

If you want to change your world, then, start by changing yourself. When you change, you transmit the changes to your world and shift the dynamic of everything in the universe. You and your circumstances are changing right now, as you read the words on this page.

In taking these steps, we change the universe of which we are part. To change your world — change yourself. The reverse is also true: when you master yourself, you master your environment.

Is Your Life in Crisis?

T his book is about starting new lives. Why do we start a new life? Because we are in crisis with our old life.

∞

Is your life in crisis? How would you know?

I ask because our crises don't always present themselves as emergencies. We usually think of crisis in big, dramatic terms — even a major positive event in our life can cause a crisis — but many crises in our lives go unrecognized, mistaken for something else. At least emergencies are obvious; they demand our immediate attention.

Most life crises are more subtle, much harder to recognize — but no less dangerous to our well-being. A seemingly tranquil life can mask an acute existential crisis.

The following questions will help you identify whether there is a crisis in your life.

- Is something important — pleasure, success, a relationship — missing in your life?
- Do you want to change something in your life, but you don't know how?
- Are you feeling "out of place" or "not yourself"? Are you feeling "stuck"?
- Are you more irritable lately with people around you?
- Are you feeling resentful about minor upsets?
- Have you suffered a loss?
- Have you had a recent change (either good or challenging) that left you feeling disoriented?
- Are you often sad?
- Do you feel overwhelmed?
- Do you remember your dreams rarely, if ever?

- Do you feel hopeless?
- Do things always seem just to go wrong?
- Are you finding it hard to imagine a satisfying future?
- Are you having nostalgic thoughts of the past?

If you answered yes to any of these questions, you may be in crisis.

Good. Crisis can be a wonderful place to begin a better life.

⁓⁓

One of my favorite client quotes is, "My life is great. *I'm the mess!*"

If the outward aspects of your life are going well — your job, your relationships, your lifestyle — but the feeling gnaws at you that something is wrong or missing, there's a good chance your life is in crisis.

Much of the pandemic depression so characteristic of modern lives stems from unexpressed crisis. The inner sources of pain, the unexplained emptiness and sadness that we experience. The dead places in our lives.

These feelings are possible signs that your life has entered a crisis stage. The places of "everything" and "nothing" are the at-risk zones for crisis in your life. Listen to what you say casually in conversation. "My marriage is all that I care about," or "I do nothing to keep in shape." Such statements are harbingers of future crises.

What Is a Crisis?

The word *crisis* derives from the ancient Greek word meaning "to decide." A crisis is a situation that compels you to make a decision. You cannot avoid a crisis by not deciding, for even deciding not to decide is a decision.

❧

The clinical term for any change that overwhelms our ability to handle it effectively, to cope, is *trauma*. We'll use the simpler word *crisis*.

A crisis can be caused by a single dramatic event or even by a series of minor assaults accumulating over a long enough time. A crisis can injure us deeply, profoundly altering the way feel about ourselves and seriously under-mining our capacity to act effectively.

❧

When a crisis occurs in one area of your life, its impact cascades into every other area. Profound change occurs like that. Let's say you've lost your job. It's not just your liveli-hood that changes — to a greater or lesser degree, *every* as-pect of your life is affected.

Change — and Crisis — Is a Part of Life

Change occurs in our lives all the time. We can generally handle these everyday changes effectively since they require only minor, incremental adaptations on our part.

Sometimes, however, a radical change occurs in our lives, one we are not equipped to handle effectively: the loss of a job, the breakup of a long-term relationship, a se-rious illness, a financial setback.

Even without abrupt upheavals, however, the daily

accumulation of changes in even the most well-ordered life creates ever-greater challenges. Eventually your old self can no longer function effectively (or experience effectively, because some people function effectively without experiencing joy).

At that point your life has reached a crisis, one whose mounting challenges will force nothing short of a revolution in your being. If that revolution does not occur, your life is cut off, especially from the opportunities around you. In short you live your life *permanently* and continually in crisis.

There are two basic systems of forward movement: evolution and revolution. Evolution consists of small, incremental changes, yet the result can be a complete metamorphosis.

Evolution eventually makes itself obsolete, and the "evolved" being no longer resembles its original structure, no longer fits into the old environment. A baby in the womb would grow too large for its maternal home and die were it not born (if he or she insisted on staying where it was) into a new world, as a new being with new challenges.

Revolution, by contrast, is sudden, shocking, and challenging. It can be thrust upon you, or you can be its catalyst. Revolution asks us to confront what we are not prepared to address. We are required to dig deep and far into ourselves to survive. We make new demands of our friends, community, and family because we have to respond, suddenly and quickly, to new and unfamiliar challenges.

After a revolution is accomplished, a cleanup often remains to be done. This cleanup is a combination of emotional, financial, physical, intellectual, and spiritual processing that can take years after the revolution, the real change, is fully accomplished.

The classic formula for dramatic fiction is to introduce a protagonist. Then force the protagonist up a tree. Then throw rocks at the stranded protagonist. Finally, give the protagonist enough resources to get down from the tree.

Notice that when the protagonist has finally come down from the tree, she has changed dramatically — and so has her world. Notice also that the protagonist will eventually find herself up another tree.

That formula is not merely the pattern for fiction — it is the pattern of our *lives.*

Things go relatively smoothly for us — seemingly, at least — from day to day. Not always without trouble, of course, but nothing we cannot handle.

But gradually, imperceptibly — or sometimes suddenly, out of nowhere — our problems accumulate to the point that we realize we are in a crisis that demands our full attention and our full resources. At that point we are up a tree, and rocks are being hurled at us.

If we recognize this process for what it is, and the lessons the universe is forcing on us, we realize that to get through the crisis *we* must change either our priorities or our behavior or our perceptions or our awareness, or perhaps all of these things.

Then the crisis passes, and we reorient ourselves to our new lives — if we have learned our lessons. Sometimes we don't learn our lessons, so we remain stuck in the same crisis or in another soon to replace it.

Exercise: Experience Break

If you were a superhero or anyone else who could resolve your crisis, who would you be?

Try that person on now. Become this hero for just a moment. Truly try this person on for size. Get up and walk around the room as this new person.

What does this person feel like inside? What are his or her skills, desires, and ways of self-expression? What do you notice when you look around as that person?

Truly pretend that this person is inside you and that you are becoming the person who can resolve your crisis. What thoughts would you have, as this person; what feelings? How would you see and experience your situation differently?

Do this exercise briefly and consistently and you will uncover skills, insights, and perspectives in yourself to guide you to a powerful resolution of your crisis. You will notice new feelings, insights, and inner shifts each time you do the exercise; the experience will change as *you* change. You are so much more than you know. You can create your dreams even if you don't know now what those dreams are.

Initially who you have to be to resolve the crisis may seem impossible to become. If your spouse has run off with someone younger, how can you be twenty again if that is who you feel you need to be to find love again? You probably can't (although I've seen some miraculous transformations). In doing this exercise, however, you will find the attributes you need in being twenty and add these qualities to the power of who you are now. This transformation doesn't happen overnight; it is a powerful ongoing process.

Consider the case of Ellen. Ellen was the headmistress of a school. Her husband found a younger, richer woman (insult to injury) and ended their twenty-year marriage. Ellen was consumed by bitterness and by the anger of her two children, who felt abandoned by both parents. In her early fifties, Ellen felt that everything she had invested in during her "beautiful" years had been taken from her. It was very hard for Ellen even to entertain doing the super-hero exercise — so she is our perfect example to illustrate how the exercise works.

LAURA: If you could be anyone who could make your life magically okay right now, who would you be?

ELLEN: Someone not so stupid as to build a life with that bastard.

LAURA: That — in your perception — is who you were. Let's go from there. Who can you be now to fix things?

ELLEN: I don't know.

LAURA: Okay, you can be someone who doesn't know. You, as your superhero, don't know. That is a courageous place to be. Someone who admits not knowing. Why don't you get up and walk around the room as someone who doesn't know. You don't know what happened, you don't know what will happen. You don't know who you are or are not. You don't know. What does this person feel like inside?

ELLEN: She feels silly walking around the room. She feels like everyone is looking at her. She feels like, since she finally has everyone's attention, she should do something good for herself with it.

LAURA: Great. Can you now say "I" instead of "she"? What do you want right now? What do you see around you?

ELLEN: I see everyone's concern. I have been feeling so ashamed. Like I am a used piece of garbage, but when I look around, not knowing, I feel like everyone wants to help me, and I am beginning to feel open to being helped. I think that I have been feeling very lonely, for a long time. Everything was caught up in trying to make Jim [her husband] happy, and that was a losing battle. I feel like I can really help other people just by being with them. I know that many of my friends have given me this feedback.

LAURA: So walk around the room as this person. Someone who has something to give and has been giving it to the wrong person for a long time. How does it feel to be this new person?

ELLEN: I feel like inviting myself to parties without waiting to be invited and making fun of my own situation. I feel like telling my children that this is just how things are and we will all figure it out together, but we have to try new things. I feel like thanking you all for inviting me and my kids into your lives, away for weekends, making my kids feel special instead of victimized by our new situation. I feel like my being stuck in what happened in my marriage is keeping me married in my heart, but bad married, sick married. When I walk around as this new person, I feel I am attractive to all of you, as if you admire my heart. I feel I can find a man who can admire this heart too even if it is in an older body. I actually feel truly beautiful right now. Now I'm embarrassed that I said that, but that's how I feel. If I think about it, I was unhappy even before he left. I needed someone who feels life as deeply as I do. My ex was all about avoiding, sports, movies, travel; everything was to avoid the very things I want. This could be my opportunity.

LAURA: So who are you as your superhero?

ELLEN: I am someone who does not know — yet who believes . . . I am someone with faith.

Notice that in doing this exercise, Ellen cited what she initially saw as failings or inabilities. The exercise showed her that even these inabilities could be turned into "super traits."

Unless we adapt ourselves to change, we can experience anger, anxiety, and possibly even depression. We can become paralyzed, frozen indefinitely in the moment between who we are and who we might become. Consider Emma's story.

For Emma, providing a certain style of life for her family meant everything. She did little else. Emma had worked at a high-profile, high-paying job for most of her marriage. She worked through the birth of her children. During their family summer vacations, she visited only on weekends. She was the primary breadwinner in their family. Her husband had worked briefly at a creative job and then stopped working completely. They had more than adequate domestic help, so her husband, although usually at home most, contributed little to the family.

Early in their marriage, Emma took pride in being able to provide for her family in ways that her parents had not been able to provide for her. Her husband, however, began to find fault with everything she did. Instead of being grateful for her sacrifice, he became resentful and abusive.

Emma clung to the idea that her family was functioning, and working was her way of contributing long after she realized she was the only one doing so. Her son became abusive to her, too, echoing his father's complaints. Her daughter was quiet and sad, not knowing how to digest the distress her mother was pretending not to experience.

Emma began to lose interest in her favorite activities. She began to lose weight. She had been a beautiful young woman, but over the years she took on an etched, haggard appearance.

One physical symptom after another appeared. Palpitations. Insomnia. Gastric problems. Female problems. She attributed her ailments to getting older. Her friends knew that her husband was having affairs, but she didn't have a clue.

Finally she found out about one of her husband's affairs. This crisis resolved years of unexpressed problems. She felt as if her life had ended and everything that she had worked for had been a waste, but her crisis allowed her to take action: she began to reclaim her children and her life.

Emma realized that providing for others was not her sole role. She realized that many elements make up a life and that she had been wasting away without them. With this in mind she began the process of rebuilding her life. She now pays attention to her distress so she can deal with its cause one day at a time. Her husband took "his share of the pie," the interest on which he will live modestly for the rest of his life.

She took all that she had earned but had not been able to enjoy — two beautiful children, a wonderful career, a capacity for genuine pleasure, and the ability to be generous in a relationship. I see the wonderful future she has awaiting her; more important, so does she.

Crisis can be a blessing in disguise. A crisis forces you to create a new life, one that responds to your deepest needs. A crisis does not allow us "to just get by," living with the rampant low-level depression of unexpressed needs and unfulfilled dreams. A crisis shakes up the status quo, spurring you to reevaluate the people and situations in your life and to make the corrections that lead to joy and success.

꙳

Crisis is transformation delayed. Not all catastrophic occurrences are easy for us to endure, of course. When we give ourselves the necessary skills and supports, however, *any* change in life can take us to a stronger and more authentic place. Authenticity means being the person who you are proud to be in a life that offers you the opportunity to express yourself fully.

A joyful life embraces crisis preparedness. The more you learn to deal with crisis, the more your life will be enhanced in all respects. Learning how to handle crises is learning how to handle life, since crises are a fundamental part of human existence.

A Crisis Can Spur Personal Growth

I am a born survivor. Even during the times that tested my resolve to live, I found myself putting one foot in front of the other, eventually regaining my stride.

When I was young I attributed my knack for survival to luck, to faith, or to my unique temperament. Yet each of these traits has failed me at times. After forty-five years of walking this planet — twenty of them working with people in crisis — I know what makes a survivor or a victim. We are all victims of something. It is what we do *after* the fall that determines whether we are also survivors.

I offer you my stories so you may see why I am so passionate about this work. The worst thing that ever happened to me turned out to be a blessing in disguise.

My Story

I love the following most about myself and in my life: My son and family. My intuition. My ability to nurture, teach, and heal others. My imagination. My caution and sensitivity. The loyal, passionate, transcendent way I love. My ability to find or create what I need in any situation.

Two days after my fourteenth birthday, my worst nightmare was realized: the only person I loved was ripped away from me. In a flash my every dream was cut short, my every belief crushed. Every structure of my life was completely upended. Yet everything I love was born that day, too.

Although I resembled my father in both my looks and my controlling, responsible nature, I was every inch my mother's daughter. I could not imagine anything or anyone more beautiful than my mother was. She inspired poetry, pictures, pride, and devotion. Even in my earliest memories, I cannot remember a time when my mother was not the center and totality of my universe. I accepted her wish to die without question. I was enthusiastically devoted to keeping her alive (I was years away from my sixteenth birthday, remember). Not once did I envy anyone else's family.

I had the most magical mother. I still remember the morning of first grade when she took me to school. I was so proud that she was mine for the world to see. Despite years of her depression, her suicide attempts, her divorce from my father, their bitter child-custody battle, my only fear was losing her, my only wish to be near her, always.

I knew that I would *always* live with my mother. I *knew*. After all, I needed her, and she needed me. My every experience was lived so I could bring it home to her and we could enjoy it together. Although the oldest of her four children, I felt as if I were the only one; certainly I was the one she lived for. I still have the letter in which she told me that I had been keeping her alive.

At the time of my mother's death, my parents were going through a difficult divorce. I was forced to live with my father, half a continent away from my mother. My father and I had a stormy relationship. I hatched new plots daily, unrelentingly thinking of ways to get back to my mother. I babysat to make money to call her where she was living with her parents in Kansas. I took as little as possible from my father so I would not become dependent on what I was going to leave. I had no time for friends or money to go to movies. I thought only of my life with my mother. Everything else was unimportant.

I had spent all my fourteen years trying to keep my mother alive. My mother, a manic-depressive, was delightful, creative, and loving when she was well or at least manic. When she was unwell, however — which was most of the time — she was agonized or suicidal or asleep.

It's odd, the details we remember years after a major life event. It was two days after my fourteenth birthday. I had been at a table-tennis tournament in Philadelphia with my good friend Squeegee and a few of our other friends. One of the boys there had facetiously yet affectionately dubbed me "jugs." His comment made me notice that I had — actually, finally — sprouted tiny breasts. I also made a new best friend at that tournament. She didn't have a mother, only a father who worked as a security guard and didn't have many teeth. I had a crush on her brother.

It was eleven o'clock at night. I had just arrived home from Philadelphia. I was tired but excited from the day. I was down at Squeegee's apartment. I was getting ready to eat a bagel when my father called and told me to come upstairs to our apartment immediately. He was at his big wooden desk in the far right-hand corner of the room. He got up from the desk as I walked in, still holding the bagel.

He was angry because I was home late. "Your mother is dead," he said. "Go take care of your brother and sisters."

In an instant, my life became surreal. I dropped the bagel and fell to the floor, not so much because I was dizzy as because I didn't know what else to do. It felt as if I were in a movie; nothing could be real in a scene in which my mother was dead.

I had spoken to her just two days earlier, on my birthday. I had been calling her all day from Philadelphia, but no one answered the phone. Usually if I couldn't get in touch with my often-suicidal mother, I would have been beside myself. On this day, however, I was so overwhelmed by my crush and my new best friend that my filial concern had wedged back into some place in my awareness that allowed me the rare opportunity to be a relatively carefree fourteen-year-old.

You might think that my world fell apart when she died, but it didn't. I kept writing her poetry, talking to her, remembering her smell as I fell asleep. I found signs of her everywhere. I simply denied that she was gone.

Then, five years later, the enormity of my loss finally

hit me one day: my mother was dead. My carefully structured world — built on the shaky foundation of denial — unraveled. So did I. Within a year I was married, had all but quit school, and was plagued by anxiety about everything from nuclear war to imagined spider veins. I was paralyzed and remained so for the following decade.

During my mother's life, I developed an exquisitely tuned intuitive ability so I could predict her depressions and suicide attempts, all in an ultimately vain attempt to keep her alive. Because my intuitive ability sometimes warned me of her episodes a little late, I also developed my healing ability: the ability to shift energy and matter for those moments. After she died, I kept fighting the same battle by becoming a healer working with the terminally ill and by becoming an intuitive as a way to anticipate, if not prevent, disaster.

In those years, I continued to look for my mother, even though I now realized she was dead. My perceptions reached so far to find her that I acquired a skill that I didn't even realize existed. My sight could go into anything — into other people, into the future, into possibilities that had not even been imagined — and describe what I saw accurately and in detail. Because of my mother's history of mental illness, I welcomed opportunities to test my intuitive and healing skills, especially queries from the scientific community. My uncanny ability became celebrated and well documented.

Years later when I went through my divorce, my intuitive ability helped me write a *New York Times* best seller that allowed other people to train their own intuition. Having spent my first fourteen years trying to heal my mother, I sought people who needed healing, gaining a worldwide reputation in the process.

My need to create my own little world that included my mother after she died has allowed me to create a safe, wonderful world for my family. My loft is the "hang-out house" for my friends and my son's friends. I work at home, in my little world, while reaching the world at large.

So you can see the worst thing that ever happened to me was indeed a blessing in disguise.

❧

My mother killed herself two days after my fourteenth birthday. Since then, I celebrate my birthday on March 22

— and commemorate my mother's death day forty-eight hours later.

I lived my childhood always on guard and at the ready. I lost my normal childhood development trying to keep my mother alive. As with all losses mine had a valuable gift hidden within it. All that I am today — the life I love, my ability to see past boundaries, my ability to heal others — derived from my childhood loss.

Nineteen years after my mother's death, almost to the day, my son was born — on my birthday.

⁂

When we experience all the crushing pain and torment of traumatic events, having the perspective to find the blessing in disguise is no easy task. When I lost my mother, it took me years to realize fully the compensations the universe had provided me.

The exercises throughout this book are designed to help you accelerate this process, so you can more fully embrace the new self, and the new life, that every crisis brings you.

Exercise: Crisis Cure

Consider the following questions:

- What do you love about your life and about yourself?
- What is the worst thing that ever happened to you?
- What would your life be like today if this event had never occurred?

Record your responses in your journal.

In the coming days and weeks, as you read this book and gain greater insight into yourself and your life, revisit these questions. You'll come to realize, as I did, that the worst thing that ever happened to you, nonetheless, brought you many of the beloved and authentic qualities in yourself and in your life.

We earn our gifts when we are forced to reach beyond who and what we are, through crisis, through loss — even through fame or good fortune that changes our lives.

When I used to tease my father about getting older (of course, he was at the time younger than I am now), he would respond by saying, "It's better than the alternative." Research has shown that the most common result of a severe trauma is not post-traumatic stress disorder — but rather substantial personal *growth*.

Crisis is our way of evolving when we lack the courage to do so on our own volition. Even if you don't buy this theory, you have no choice but to move forward in your life. The important questions are not "Why did this happen to me?" or "How did this happen?" but rather "What am I?" and "Where do I want to go with what I have now?" Your answer may be "I want to go back to my marriage" or "I want to be the person I was before I was mugged," or "before my mother died" or, or, or . . .

You can find fulfillment in another fashion — if you go to the root of what you are truly missing and remember that much regret is guilt. We torture ourselves with the childhood fantasy that we control the world and if we had only done this or that we wouldn't be in the pain we are in right now.

When I lost my mother, yes of course, I wanted her

back. The root of what I wanted, however, was to feel as connected to another human being who looked at me with the love and care as I looked upon my mother.

Crisis is a violent blow to your world. When your life reaches a crisis, you have no choice: you evolve, or you remain crippled.

Survival is not simply the ability to continue breathing. Survival is the ability to transform every crisis or change into a more powerful, effective, and satisfying life. Survival is the ability to give up what you were so you can evolve into someone more joyous and luminous.

Endings are beginnings — if we allow them to be. Because we find it so hard to let go, however, bringing ourselves to a better place is uncertain.

Living is about learning how to let go of things — fears and dreams and people and situations — in order to get to a better place.

We see our lives as having linear paths. Consider our occupations. The word *career* derives from older words meaning "road" and, later, "racecourse."

With this notion of life, we should not be surprised at the stark terror each of us feels when that career seems hurtling — or limping — out of control or when our lives feel increasingly "off course."

The truth is far different. Our lives are actually a succession of ever-expanding cycles in which we exchange one self and life for another.

What gets us into trouble is when we don't recognize the process, and we fight it all the way.

✌

Remember: crisis is an opportunity for dramatic, positive change. Things are *supposed* to fall apart, to bring you to a better place. Those who don't see life that way remain stuck in endings.

A New Life Awaits, So Long as You Give Up Your Old

A few years ago I sat alone in a café near the Museum of Natural History here in New York City, savoring a cup of tea. It was early February, usually the dead of freezing winter, and most certainly not my favorite time of year.

This particular winter, however, had been remarkably warm. So warm, in fact, that it seemed as if the winter had not yet begun and that New York had been basking in a mild fall.

I was enjoying the view of the museum and the

passers-by through the café's large windows when my attention was arrested by a peculiar sight. The deciduous tree immediately outside my seat in the café still had all of its leaves (remember, this was midwinter).

It dawned on me that because the tree had not experienced sufficiently cold temperatures throughout the fall and early winter, it had not "known" to relinquish its leaves. I was panged by the realization that in a matter of weeks, with the approach of spring, new buds would try to emerge from the tree's normally leafless branches.

How, I wondered, would the tree resolve its dilemma? How could new life emerge from the branches as long as the tree clung to pieces of its old life?

I still think of this tree from time to time, especially when I contemplate how often we individuals cling to old parts of ourselves whose time has past and, in doing so, prevent newer, more vital parts of our being from emerging.

To live life and to make the many transitions our lives require, we must master the ability consciously to let go of an old reality and be ready to create a new one. The new life you build is the gift of transmuting crises into blessings.

৵

As embryos, we gain perception and power only slowly. At first, we are without any consciousness of experience because the brain does not develop until a certain number of months of gestation. Slowly our limbs, organs, and perceptions include an awareness of our being.

At some point after conception, we gain the ability to direct our actions consciously and to adapt to our environment in new ways. As soon as we are able to do this, our environment (the womb) becomes cramped, and we secrete the necessary hormones to be born.

In being born, we leave behind everything we have known or experienced. We allow many of our adapting mechanisms to become obsolete because we are uncomfortable and must make change. In fact, if we continue to remain in the uterine environment past our time, we are never born into a new world. We die.

The baby in the womb is, then, *reborn* at birth, breathing air, having to communicate for food, warmth, and safety. Once you have experienced the loss of what was — the loss of the "self" you were within the womb — there is no going back. The situation that was — the you that was — exists no longer.

There is no going back; that is the tragedy of being human. There is, however, always a going *forward*; that is the divine gift and privilege of being human.

꙳

The aim of our lives should be to climb higher above the pile of our experiences into the newer, stronger, more brilliant, more joyful, more wonderful selves we are meant to be. Yet we hold on — to good experiences as well as bad — and in doing so we stay stuck.

Letting Go Is Hard

To live fully you must be willing to let go of your self. That task is never easy, for no matter how dysfunctional our old life may have been, it defined us, and we were defined by it.

Letting go of the past is the most difficult part of being human. All that you identify as "self" and as "home" is contained in your history.

Yet life presents you with situations that demand surrender — or else. You may not always know that a relationship is over, that it is right to leave a job, a town, even to leave a way of seeing yourself. Consider Jaime's story.

When Jaime was twelve, his mother died. When his father died a year later, he and his younger brother were placed in foster care. One family on Long Island offered to take both boys.

Although both brothers had been deeply attached to their father and, of course, to being a family, they responded to the crisis in very different ways. Chris, a year younger than Jaime, exploded every time a new experience was introduced. He resisted changing schools, he resented his foster family, he insisted on coming back to the city for entertainment even though there was plenty available on Long Island. He failed to make new friends and was often truant from school, hanging out in the city with his old gang. Understandably, he clung to the trappings of a life now lost. He went from foster home to foster home, never settling in anywhere. Last I heard of him, he was in jail.

Jaime worked hard to fit into his new family. He joined the soccer team even though his city-boy game had been chess. He knew that he never again wanted to be in the situation he was currently in, as a guest in someone else's home. He focused his energy on getting the grades that would get him into a good college. He learned about opportunities that were available to foster children from the state and made the most of them. He had a new status, and he used every opportunity that it offered.

It wasn't until he was through college, in a career, married, and expecting his own first child (all of which he did very young) that he experienced the full impact of his grief. When this happened, however, he had a home of his own, a loving wife, and a new life on the way. He was able to count his blessings as he mourned his loss.

Chris could not let go of his past. He remains a boy, beloved by his parents, living in New York City. That little boy is still looking to find a home in a past that no longer exists. He was unable to become the person who could capitalize on new circumstances.

Jaime put one foot in front of the other and moved on. He observed, changed, adapted, managed his behavior, and found his way "back home" to a family of his own. To do that he had to let go of a way of being and a life that he deeply loved but the attachment to which could cause him only harm.

৯

Learning to live well means learning to let go. That knowledge and ability make us joyful and successful.

We all realize the importance of giving up harmful things in our lives: a bad relationship, a debilitating job. But relinquishing even these things is often impossible until you let go of the sense of self that is bound up with these things.

Surprisingly, your ability to give up one sense of yourself for another is a skill you have used since childhood. We spend much of our childhood developing our pragmatic knowledge of self. We learn to know who our families are, what our rules are, what our responsibilities are, what our beliefs are, and so on. We learn who we are in the world.

At each succeeding stage of our life, we are forced to give up that sense of self and begin anew the process of re-defining just who we are. Adolescence. Adulthood. Parenthood. Old age. At each chapter in our lives, we must begin the never-ending quest to answer that simple question: *Who am I?*

We all understand why Peter Pan wanted to remain young forever, and yet Peter Pan never experienced the many joys that come with maturity.

We Must Learn to Let Go

At all levels — as individuals, as companies, as a society — we work with change ineffectively because we think of ourselves as durable structures that undergo only evolutionary changes. We often resist change — attempting desperately to hold on to what we used to have — to maintain our illusion of control.

To reassure ourselves of this illusory control, we often try to rebuild or heal the old instead of moving on. Moving on does not always mean leaving. I have known many relationships that died and, yet, were reborn as something different yet lasting.

ॐ

In our society we are not taught to handle life's major transitions. "There are no second acts in American lives," lamented the author F. Scott Fitzgerald. So we resist change in pathological and ultimately futile ways.

To have a second act, you need to close the curtain on the first act.

That's the catch.

As you read this book, you are raising the curtain on the next act of your life.

ॐ

I know people who have remained stagnant in selves that have grown obsolete. Experiences that would have thrown the hardiest of us into crisis have passed over them and left them unchanged. This may seem enviable, especially for those currently going through the painful part of crisis in this moment. These people, however, never grow.

If you do not grow, like the baby outgrowing its

womb, you stagnate. This stagnation often takes the form of illness, depression, weight problems, and worse.

If you are not an active participant in your own life, then you are its victim. This point is illustrated in Thea's story.

Thea was a beautiful, successful, forty-two-year-old woman. A friend brought her to one of my workshops to learn to develop her intuition. Thea was recovering from a broken heart. A few months prior, Thea had met the man whom she thought she would marry. They were together every minute, and he had all but moved into her apartment. She couldn't understand why he suddenly turned cold and distant toward her and then broke up with her.

As Thea's story unfolded, I realized that her relationships were all the same. She would meet a man, he would fall madly in love with her, and then she with him. As she got closer to her dream of having a family, she would become anxious and needy, and the relationship would soon end. By that point she was so focused on "sealing the deal" that the relationship was no longer satisfying to her, either. In her twenty-five-year relationship history, her behavior in every relationship had been the same.

Her parents, who had been together for more than twenty years, could not understand why their beautiful and talented daughter was alone. Thea had enjoyed the text-book normal childhood. Two significant elements in her story emerged, however. She had been the youngest child who competed with two older siblings for attention. It was also clear that she was an anxious responder. When she be-came attached in a romantic relationship and afraid to "lose her place," her anxiety would take over (with under-tones of anger).

Instead of challenging her behavior and dealing with her anxiety, Thea simply repeated the pattern of her love drama with each new partner. She continued to find lovers, so her situation never reached the full-blown crisis stage that would have forced her to examine her pattern. The considerable pain that she experienced in her love life was not enough to force change. She remained stagnant, alter-nating between hope and dejection.

Attachment Is Okay, So Long as You Can *Unattach*

When I speak of the need for every human being to be willing to let go, I am not suggesting that you adopt a stoic indifference to what you have. Far from it: you must be attached to something in order to let it go.

All religions teach the importance of not being too attached to worldly things, whether to our possessions or our hopes or even those around us. It is important to be passionately attached to whatever is going on in the moment — but it is equally important to be able to acknowledge when a situation has changed, or when *you* have changed, and the beloved, trusted structures, relationships, and situations in your life are no longer the same.

Nonattachment, then, is the position of attention in which you are your own teacher, when you can look at the present moment from a new perspective.

Letting go — *while* keeping what you truly need. *That's* the challenge.

How do you know it's time to let go? Sometimes the question is harder when you know it's time to let go, but you don't know *what* to let go of!

Keep in mind that when you judge yourself for your more petty or "unenlightened" conflicts, you ignore an inner metaphor that can hold great power. What you feel needs to be addressed and criticized.

The Grand Cycle of Self

We think of journeys as having a beginning and an end. In reality journeys are circles, part of one forming the doorway to the next cycle, endings and beginnings happening simultaneously in every moment. Life itself is a circle with no beginning and no end. And loss and crisis are inherent, inescapable parts of life's continuum.

By creating a new self, I mean more than simply "reinventing" yourself. For a complete rebirth to occur, a person must be experiencing a crisis on all levels: an emotional crisis, a physical crisis — in her environment as well as her body — and especially a crisis of faith.

Re-creating yourself is your birthright. For your new, brilliant self to emerge, you must embrace loss — mourn it, but also celebrate the doorways loss opens for you. When you accept the inevitability of loss, you liberate your latent self. There are many people you might have become had fear, shame, or circumstances not guided you in another direction. These selves can still emerge.

᷂

Life is full of loss. Everything we are, everything we know, changes as regularly as the seasons. Some of these losses are predictable, the organic culminations of growth. At other times our lives as we know them are snatched from us with the death of a spouse, a crime against us, or the loss of our health or livelihood.

You're trying to hold on, but life has told you that your old self is ready to move on to make room for your new self to emerge. We either embrace loss and live fully or deny and resist it, condemning ourselves to mourn eternally.

Revisit the Question of Self Frequently

 Awareness is a powerful agent of change. Your focus has already shifted in subtle ways from the crisis to a new, more powerful way of being. Your sense of self has also begun to shift in positive ways. It will continue to evolve as you work through this book, and beyond. From time to time, then, whenever the inspiration strikes you, reconsider that most fundamental of all questions: *Who are you?*

How Do You Respond
to Change?

How you respond to change in your life is as important as what kind of change occurs.

By the time you feel the need to make a change in your life, the change has *already* occurred! What has not yet occurred is your *response* to that change.

Change itself isn't hard; acknowledging and accepting the change that has already occurred in your life is.

so

Change can be an effective tool to take you to the next level of joy, productivity, creativity, and success. Change can also stun you into inaction, into a destructive reaction, or injure the core of your belief in your world and in yourself. The difference is not in the kinds of changes that happen to you, but in the ways you perceive these changes and respond to them.

৯৹

There are many ways of adapting to change. Some of these are nourishing, and some of them are injurious. Many people adapted as children by removing themselves from life — not in fact being affected by the world and relationships around them because they remove themselves from responding to it. Of course, these same people are lonely, isolated, and often ineffective in many areas of their lives.

To be effective in your life, you need to have the capacity to be affected by events, and to grow from your experiences rather than being derailed by them. People who adapt to change organically, without trauma, have the capacity to experience loss, yet possess the intuition and process that enable them to create from the void.

These people are open to the changes in their lives without letting these changes determine who they are and whom they've chosen to become. They are self-directed and capable of responding to their environment in healthy and innovative ways. We recognize these individuals by their warmth, imagination, and integrity. Every decade they seem to have reinvented themselves and their lives. They do not fear crisis because they live their dreams, realizing that any difficulties they encounter lead to successful new beginnings.

≈

We all resist life's changes in our own way. No matter how authentic your life is, you will at times resist change. What is your resistance type? I have my habitual ways of resisting changes; so do you. Some people respond to change with denial; others with fear or rage; others are stunned into inaction or frenetic, ineffective action.

Becoming acquainted with the ways you respond to and resist change is essential. Once you know your personal tendencies around change, you can begin anticipating and avoiding the predictable pitfalls you are predisposed to.

To deal with change effectively, you need to go through a predetermined, ritualized process. Having the process organized for you in steps, as I do in this book, will enable you to overcome your resistance to change no matter how you seek to avoid that change.

≫

My sister is fond of saying that we all have our own Everest to climb, but for each of us it is a different mountain. When crisis hits, each person crashes into her own weakness and is haunted by her own version of pain.

Crisis tends to bring out our conditioned responses to a heightened degree. If you tend to panic, your fear becomes disorganizing. If you tend to rage, your anger becomes alienating. It is important to know how you are prone to react to crisis so you can tend to yourself and your needs in specific and targeted ways. Right now you do not have extra reserves to allow for mistakes with yourself or the safety of the world around you.

Identifying your type can help you stay on the path to strength.

Exercise: Packing Your Trunk

A classic children's memory game — that adults can play, too — goes like this. The first player completes the following sentence: "I packed my grandmother's truck and in it I put ———."

So, for example, the first player might say, "I packed my grandmother's trunk and in it I put *an apple.*" The next player repeats the sentence and adds another item to the list, as in, "I packed my grandmother's truck and in it I put an apple and a bear." And so on.

As the list grows, players have an increasingly difficult task reciting all the items. The first person to forget something in the trunk loses the game, and the next round starts afresh.

We'll play our own variation of this classic. Pack *your* trunk — what do you want to take with you into your new life?

As you take stock of what you have, you may find that many of the contents of your trunk were added by someone else or by situations that no longer exist. Do you really want to pack the big house that eats all of your money now that your children have left home? Do you pack being the only breadwinner or always having a girlfriend or being the helper for everyone's problems? You can pack things, people, situations, or ways of being.

You are allowed to pack only things that you actually have. You can't pack something you have lost. However, as you work through this book, you can add things to your trunk. Look at your trunk regularly to see if you can take something out or if you have acquired something new in the process of change that you want to take with you.

If you can, record this exercise on paper and redo it every time you feel the need to sort things out in your life. The ritual of doing this exercise will help you intellectually and subconsciously see and effectively use the resources that you have right now.

There are four basic types of response to dramatic change in our lives. The following quiz will help you identify your type or response type. Once you've identified how you typically respond to change, you can apply my suggestions for handling each type.

Take your time and be honest. You may find it helpful to get the outside perspective of a good friend — especially if you are a denial type!

Identifying How You Respond to Change

Check off the statements below that apply to you. You may find that you display characteristics of more than one type, but you will identify most with one primary set of feelings and behaviors.

Depression

- Do you have trouble taking pleasure in things you used to enjoy?
- Do you isolate yourself?
- Do you find yourself thinking repeatedly about your troubles or difficulties?
- Are you more tired than usual? Do you find it difficult to complete ordinary, day-to-day tasks?
- Have you lost interest in caring for your personal appearance?

- Do you cry frequently and uncontrollably?
- Do you want the world just to go away?

Anxiety

- Are you unusually forgetful?
- Are your actions frenetic, impulsive, and ineffective?
- Do you have the feeling that things just can't wait?
- Do you repeat yourself often?
- Do you have trouble sleeping or awaken in the middle of the night?
- Do you have an insatiable need for reassurance?
- Have your eating patterns changed significantly? Do you eat too much or too little?
- Do you feel like you are going to jump out of your skin?

Rage

- If you are a woman, do you feel like you have PMS all the time? If you are a man, do you find yourself often holding back physical responses to others?
- Do you find yourself snapping or even exploding at people more frequently?

- Do you instantly develop road rage?
- Do you feel a need to respond to every irritation?
- Do you find yourself having revenge or other violent fantasies?
- Do you hurt yourself or others?
- Do you feel like everyone in your life is failing you?

Denial

- Are you becoming superman or superwoman at your job or in the home?
- Are you cutting off people's attempts to offer you help or sympathy?
- Do you keep your emotions in check, rarely losing your temper, never crying or yelling?
- Do you never allow thoughts of the crisis to intrude?
- Do you go out of your way to not be seen by others as vulnerable?
- Do you find yourself cut off from all creative outlets such as painting, writing, singing, fantasizing?
- Do you avoid people who see your situation differently than you do, especially old friends?

As I mentioned earlier, you may find aspects of yourself in all four types, but one type should predominate. You probably have a "knee-jerk" type that is the first mode you go into when dealing with overwhelming stress. Although under stress you will most likely fall first into your primary reactive type, you will have moments in all four types.

Now that you have identified how you tend to respond to change and crisis, the following prescriptions, done regularly, will take the disruptive energy of crisis and channel it toward what you want to create next in your life.

Understanding the Depressed Responder

The depressed responder often felt helpless as a child. All of this child's efforts could not change the difficulties in his or her environment; what's worse, this child had the depth to be aware of this futility.

If your response type is depression, chances are that just when you need to move into action, your energy deserts you, leaving you unable to respond to life's demands. Someone probably gave you this book. You wish that you had it on tape because you aren't particularly interested in reading anything, including what I have to say. You do not feel that your efforts will come to anything, and even if they would, you don't have the energy to make them. You are probably having trouble imagining a life where you would be happy. Nothing, not even your own future, interests you very much anymore.

Right now you need to make tiny moves toward self-support. Do not undertake all of the suggestions I am giving you at once. You are where you are right now. Take the suggestions that are easiest for you, and try them out.

Put the phone next to the couch and call anyone you know who can offer any kind of support right now. Better yet, start by having a friend make those calls for you. Support includes, but is not limited to, bringing food over, helping you at work, being responsible for your mail and check writing, gathering information about resources that can help your current situation.

Your task is to create more comfort for yourself. You need to keep your focus on what you can do now. Don't wander into the past or the future. You have no objectivity now for that to be a comforting experience. In depression your physical system needs adequate sleep, rest, and nourishment. Follow a comforting daily routine. Go to work, eat meals, and maintain positive habits and activities. Even a little bit of exercise, perhaps dancing to a song on the radio, goes a long way to lifting your system out of a depressed state. Altering your environment can snap you out of a depressive pattern. If you can, go on vacation, get a massage, or see a friend who makes you laugh.

Depression does not define you. The voice of depression often sounds quite reasonable. It can tell you that you are now seeing reality for the first time, or that this is just how you are and you will feel this way forever no matter what you do. It is the voice of despair. By treating the symptoms of depression, you enable yourself to move forward toward your new life.

If your response type is depression, your gift is depth. When you resolve your depression, your profundity will remain.

Understanding the Anxious Responder

The anxious responder felt overwhelmed as a child. Too much was going on that this child had to respond to, and she was always on guard to address tasks that she was too young to handle.

If your response type is anxiety, you probably find it hard to focus on this page. You are in physical and psychological readiness for the next blow to occur. You may think the same thoughts repeatedly. You may be finding it hard to eat, or you may be eating compulsively. You may be impulsive right now: saying things without thinking, buying things that you don't want or need, or fearfully refusing to buy yourself things that you really need. You may be making phone calls in the middle of the night looking for someone to understand you or help you take action. Your body may be full of tension, so you are uncomfortable even when you sleep. You can't stop thinking, but your thoughts bring you no resolution and no relief. Your pulse may be rapid when you go to bed and when you wake up in the morning. You may find that you are disorganized and are drawing a mental blank in situations that used to be second nature for you.

Your task is to engage in activities that lower your anxiety a little bit each day. Find consuming activities: play with your child, make love to your spouse, take a brisk walk or an aerobics class. If you can be still long enough for a massage, get a deep one that will work through the stress kinks anxiety has given you. Simplify your daily routine. Make a checklist so you can keep track of your day. Put reminders up to breathe deeply. Scream to your favorite song until you are exhausted. Whenever you feel your body tighten and your mind going around in circles, interrupt the process by shifting your focus to an activity. Find the places where you can get lost in experience. Read. Zone out in front of the television. Go bicycle riding with your friends.

This is not a time to think things through. You will tend toward dire outcomes, worst-case scenarios, which will, of course, step your anxiety up a notch. Avoid stimulants, including coffee and tea. Eat on a regular schedule. Do not allow anxiety to freeze you into inactivity and panic. When you are about to do something impulsive, look at it from the other person's point of view. Would you like to be awakened at midnight or reminded to do something five times in two hours? Unlike someone with depression, you have too much energy now, and it needs an outlet. Throw yourself into your work. Exercise. Do creative projects. Find support to approach the situations that make you anxious. Avoidance heightens anxiety. Channel

that anxious energy into something satisfying and productive. This may be your chance to repaint every room in
your house. When your anxiety is managed, you will see
what now seems insurmountable as far more manageable.

If your response type is anxiety, your gift is awareness.
When you have calmed your anxiety, your acuity and insight will remain.

Understanding the Enraged Responder

The rageful responder felt powerless as a child. This child
was often roughly treated or had his or her need for protection denied. The feelings and events of the child's form-
ative years were overpowering in some intrinsic way.

If your response type is rage, you will be angered by at
least one thing I say before this paragraph is complete. Ex-
pressing your anger does *not* make it better. Anger feeds
anger, and when you express your anger while still hot, you
fuel it, biochemically and intellectually. Feeling will find
reason to justify its own existence. If you have an anger
type, you want to soothe the beast and not inflame it.

Rage can complicate your relationships and alienate
your supporters at a time when you need them the most.

Find an acceptable outlet for the rage. Try sports, writing, hitting a pillow. Identify the triggers that flame the rage and learn to change your response. If certain people call you and make you furious, stop speaking to them. If on the way to work you walk past the apartment that you shared with your ex-husband, alter your route.

Don't bottle up your rage. Let it out in a way that doesn't hurt you or others. If you feel explosive, remove yourself from the situation. Get to know your early anger cues so you can interrupt the process before it takes hold of you. Curse in the shower; draw pictures; jog five miles. Use fantasy to re-create rage-inducing experiences — yet alter your habitual responses and the predictable outcomes. Cultivate positive fantasy.

Stop blaming. Pretend it really is your entire fault and only you can make it better. Use your creativity as you never have before, whether through art, dance, or cooking. These outlets will give you the tools to express your feelings in an effective and healing way.

If your response type is anger, your gift is passion. When you are not using your juice on rage, your passion for life will remain.

Understanding the Denying Responder

The child who responded with denial had too much information or intrusion to process and understand comfortably. This child found ways to escape through activity and
mastering the things in the world that could be mastered.

If your response type is denial, you are probably reading this book to help someone else. Everything is fine
with you, even though things that are essential for other
people — a relationship, free time, pleasure — may not
be in your life, right? You have kept your feelings and
responses under such tight control that you no longer
know what they are. You have some feeling of not having
any intimate relationships or communication in your life,
but you are too busy to think about it.

You'll know that you are the denial type if something
has happened in your life that would floor most people,
but it hasn't even fazed you. You don't think about it or
mourn your loss; you simply move on. Not experiencing
the pain of crisis may sound wonderful, but in order to
move on, you have to keep people, experiences, and even

your own feelings at such a distance that your world becomes a lonely place.

Your task is to feel all of your feelings and acknowledge your experiences in small, safe ways. Structure periods
of your day when you can take a glimpse at your feelings.
Cry in a movie, listen to a song that reminds you of your
loss, work to expand your emotional range by being with
people who elicit an emotional part of you that you don't
ordinarily feel. (Who are these people? Chances are they
are precisely the people you have been avoiding lately.)

Look for the child within you who was incapable of
using denial; listen to what she needs and what she has
to say. Listen to other people, especially those who have
experienced the same kind of crisis or pain. Know that
when you feel the pain, it won't be forever, and the pain
that you are not feeling is blocking many other satisfying
and joyful emotions with it. Know that most people want
to know you and do not want to judge you. Chances are
that they have had similar pain in their lives. Know that
when you can feel who you are, you will fall in love with
yourself.

If your response type is denial, your gift is competence. Once you work through the denial, the competence will remain.

◦

When you manage your response type, you take an enormous step toward gaining mastery over any situation. Your response type comes from a lifetime of patterning. If any of these conditions persist, it may be helpful to consult a doctor or otherwise qualified professional.

Many people look upon medication as a crutch. On the other hand, some of our response type is biological — genetically patterned into how our bodies and brains work, especially under stress. Sometimes pharmaceutical intervention can break the pattern enough to help you get a grip on the challenges that confront you.

I have given you behavioral techniques that should be helpful and, if used regularly, will also restructure how your brain and body respond to stress. As with all of life, the support of your family, friends, and community will help you make the changes you need to move to the next step in your personal evolution.

❧

Once you've mastered your reactive type, you've gained considerable mastery over yourself.

- If you are an anxiety type, you will know that you are mastering your type when you can experience periods of denial. Denial allows anxiety types time to organize and cope.
- If you are an anger type, you will know that you are mastering your type when you can experience periods of depression. Depression allows the anger type to stop acting on impulse and to process the situation in a more profound way.
- If you are a denial type, you will know that you are mastering your type when you can experience anxiety. Anxiety forces the denial type to confront the feelings and conflicts of the situation, creating better decision making and the opportunity for integration.
- If you are a depression type, you will know that you are mastering your type when you are moved to anger. Anger allows depression types to mobilize

and generate their energy outwardly instead of inwardly.

To defend against the forward movement of healing — and there is a strong pull to remain in type — you may experience the following reactions:

- Anxiety types are defending against the hopelessness of depression.
- Denial types are defending against the pain of rage.
- Rage types are defending against the helplessness of anxiety.
- Depression types are defending against the discernment and demands of denial.

✧

Your type keeps you isolated, insulated, and stagnant. As you master your type, you allow time to perform its miraculous feats of healing.

Time lessens the impact of the initial crisis. Time allows you the opportunity to explore different options. Time allows personality and presentation to adapt to the new circumstances. Time allows your actions and decision making to adapt to the new circumstances. Time allows you to come up with new and appropriate dreams, wishes, and goals. Time allows you to view your world from a new perspective, revealing new opportunities.

If you are an anxiety type and time is not working for you, stop interfering and controlling and allow time to do its thing. If you are an anger type and time is not working for you, stop picking at your own wounds and allow time to create restitution. If you are a depression type and time is not working for you, it is because you are so lost in your inactivity and seclusion that you are not responding to the opportunities that time presents or allowing for the evolution of self that time allows. If you are a denial type and missing the benefits of time, it is because you are closing off your options by denying the recognition of change and, therefore, missing the possibilities that are occurring.

- If you are a denial type, chances are that you don't often see the crisis coming.
- If you are an anger type, you probably create most of your crises by destabilizing situations through rage.

- If you are an anxiety type, you are so busy dealing with problems that don't really exist or matter that the real situations in your life grow to crisis proportions.
- If you are a depression type, you probably let your problems pile up, retreating from appropriate actions even when you know what actions to take, until situations truly are at a crisis point.

You have a choice. Depression types can direct their profound understanding to the people and situations around them and elicit the support for action. Denial types can efficiently and effectively deal with the realities of a situation once they allow themselves to see it. Anxiety types can use their discernment to choose what to focus on and when to act. Anger types can use their passion to create and devote themselves to new ways of being.

Remember that each response type has a unique gift that can create true meaning, joy, and success in your new life. The most important benefit of working with your type is the ability to take care of business effectively.

I will have more to say on these different response types throughout the book, especially in chapter 11, where I'll discuss how to recognize these response types in others going through crisis. Sometimes helping others through their crises helps us recognize how we ourselves handle losses in our lives.

A Whole New World: Taking Your First Steps

Embrace Where You Are

The sooner you deal with your new set of realities, the more quickly you will move to a place of strength and action. Where you are right now may not feel good to you, but you have to deal with what is real and what is left for you to work with. You may have some good surprises. Maybe your hopes of "if only this would happen" will come true. For the moment, however, you can work only with what is, in this moment.

Even if you could walk right back into your old life at its best, it would not be the same. *You* are different. People with good childhoods or wonderful high-school careers or great beauty in their youth often think, "If only I could go back."

The you who lived that life no longer exists. You can never go back; if you are going forward with conscious direction, you won't want to.

The consciously lived life creates the ideal situation for each stage of your development. Often a crisis is generated precisely because your unconscious and your intuition know that you need to grow in order to emotionally and spiritually survive, but you just can't stop hanging on.

Don't beat yourself up. We are biologically programmed to avoid change. Any animal will immediately be on guard when any change is introduced into its environment. Thankfully, you are more than your unconscious, instinctive brain. You have the ability to direct your life.

You need to embrace who you are and where you are right now. It may not be where you want to be. Your worst fear may be remaining this person stuck in the current reality. In order to gain sufficient traction to move forward, though, you need to have your tires firmly in the dirt. Remind yourself that you have the power to take yourself *wherever* you need to go — even if you don't know where that is right now.

Your task right now is not omniscience. Your task is simply to extend one foot in front of the other and walk.

So

One of the advantages of true, earthshaking crisis is that it is hard to hold on to an extinct way of being. Crisis rarely happens in such cataclysmic proportions, however. In the absence of having your patterns ripped away, you need to be disciplined about avoiding tunnel vision and the repetition of useless-yet-seductive behaviors.

Consciously avoid looking for old landmarks to tell you where you are. You are in a new country now. If you feel calm only when you are shut in your house, go outside. If you continually seek reassurance from others, go through a day in which you are your only source of comfort. If you bottle things up until you explode, try raising your heart rate once an hour by doing jumping jacks.

Denial types have a difficult road because they are rarely aware of their patterns, or don't believe they have them in the first place. If you scored as a denial type on the test, you need to expand your awareness of the world around you, as well as of yourself. Begin by creating a library of feeling. Gather things that evoke feeling — art, music, poetry, photos — and once an hour take one minute out to stop, breathe, and *feel*.

The new people and experiences that come into your life will be . . . well, new. You probably won't feel immediately comfortable with the positive and enlightening changes that may already have happened from the time that you opened this book. Rare is the person who feels immediately "at home" in a new situation and having to respond in new ways.

I remember when I first met my current boyfriend more than a decade ago. I was making all of the usual comparisons between him and my ex. As I was going down the list, I said, "He feels so different. Our relationship isn't what I am used to." My friend gave me one of those "when-was-your-lobotomy?" looks of incredulity and said, "Uh, this is a *good* thing!"

Apply First Aid to Your Life

If you are in a crisis right now, take the following steps. When you are on the other side of this crisis, you can read the rest of the book so you can avoid ever finding yourself in this position again. Act as if you have power in this situation, even if you don't feel that this is true right now, by doing the following things. I will go into them in further depth later in this chapter. For now, know that this is your new to-do list. This, and only this, is where your attention needs to be focused.

- Focus on the present. Your only power is in the present. You cannot change the past, and it is a waste of time to extend your crisis into a future that isn't here yet. Stay focused on the present.
- Give your crisis a name. Every crisis has a community. Allow people who have experienced similar crises and have the information, resources, and collective strength to help you.
- Have a goal, even a minor one. You need a direction

that moves you away from crisis. Allow this goal to change as you gain strength.

- Know who you have to be in this crisis. What do you have to know, what actions do you have to take, to carry you to safety?

- Use intuition to take you in the right direction, even when you do not consciously know where the right direction is.

- Be aware of how you usually react to crisis and use the tools in chapter 4 to do things differently this time around.

- Use your sleep state to process the crisis and anchor you in solutions. Write down your challenges before you go to sleep so you can use your downtime to organize and integrate.

- Identify the community that can support you through this crisis; find mentors to help you.

- No matter what you are feeling right now, know that this chapter in your life, too, shall end and that you can choose the next chapter.

- Remember all of the times that you successfully

navigated crisis (if you are still standing, you have done so before) and reassure yourself that you can do it again.

Start right now to do the things on your survival list. Even minor healthy adaptations to your new self and your new world will grow into the fertile ground of your future.

We'll discuss these steps in more detail throughout this chapter. For now, consider Harry's story.

One day Harry's ex-wife appeared in San Francisco with their four-year-old daughter, Ellie, and a suitcase and told him that she needed time on her own. Harry and his wife had split up when his daughter was eight months old. Harry had moved to San Francisco, and although he had made twice-yearly trips to visit his daughter in Boston, he had never been on his own with her for more than a few hours. His ex said that she would call in a few days and leave a number. Harry was furious, and they got into a screaming fight before she walked out, mother and daughter hugging good-bye and crying. Normally Harry would have put his fist through the wall and then gone out and

WELCOME TO YOUR CRISIS

gotten drunk. What he did in the next twenty-four hours surprised Harry as well as everyone who knew him.

Harry had been dating a woman whom he liked very much. He called her for advice. She let him know in no uncertain terms that she wanted nothing to do with a child or with him until he got the situation resolved. His daughter was sitting on the couch of his studio apartment and hadn't moved since her mother had left. He went over and sat down next to her and into a puddle of urine that had spread on the cushion beneath her. In the space of an hour, he had gained a daughter, lost a girlfriend, and landed in a whole new world. He didn't even know if four-year-olds changed themselves or had to be changed. He looked at his daughter and said, "That happens to me all of the time." She burst into tears, and he held her, wet and shaking, until she fell asleep.

He removed her wet clothes, wrapped her in a soft blanket, and placed her on his bed. Then he e-mailed everyone he trusted, asking for help. Every time he panicked or felt his rage building — which according to him, was every few minutes — he looked at his e-mail and followed another suggestion. One mother suggested that he unpack her suitcase and make her a little place of her own right away. Someone e-mailed him about a social club comprised solely of single parents. Another person sent information about a single-dad support group. Ellie awakened at five in the morning. On three hours' sleep he was irritable and feeling helpless. He forgot to call in to work, a job that he had recently gotten after a few lean months.

His supervisor called him. Harry said he was sick. His supervisor clearly did not believe him, so Harry called back and leveled with him. His supervisor was not interested in hearing the story. Harry knew he couldn't lose his job, so he called a friend who had a child around the same age and asked for babysitting help.

He cleaned himself up, went to work, let his supervisor know that he had resolved the problem and it would not happen again (without telling him what he really thought of him), and simply didn't allow himself to be fired. After work he picked up his daughter, made a to-do list, ordered fast food, and got them both to bed before nine. When he put his head on the pillow, he was so angry he couldn't fall asleep. So he got up, did fifty push-ups, took a shower, found some more e-mail offers of help, looked at his beautiful, sleeping daughter, really his for the first time in her life, and went to sleep. When he woke up in the morning, he thought, "I am a father. I can do this. I did it yesterday, I can do it today."

In other words he put one foot in front of the other and went steadily forward.

Get Your Bearings

Am I safe? Am I whole? Is anybody there?

If you are in crisis, these questions need to be addressed immediately. You may not get the answers, but you will begin on the road to safety.

When your self and your world are in tumult, confusion is unavoidable. If you reach for old tools, behaviors, and life structures, however, you will have difficulty surviving in new terrain. You need to assimilate into a new order and find what you need to grow in new ways.

The world is unfamiliar to you, and you are unfamiliar to yourself. You've lost or had to abandon many of the tools, supports, and other securities you had before your new self began to emerge.

⚮

Assimilation is an ongoing process, one that is nourishing even when we are not in a moment of beginning. Once you have begun the process of creating safety in your environment, you can attend to learning who you — the you in this moment — are. You don't need the long answer to this question right now. You need the short form: just enough for you to begin to function effectively again.

Safety First

Although you may not feel safe right now, you need to act as your own good parent. Basic needs such as nourishment, shelter, support, expression, and comfort must be simplified and attended to before you can safely move into your new world.

What is safety? The basic and minimum requirements for the protection of life constitute safety. If you are too anxious to function effectively on your own, seek help. Achieving safety may require exercising, getting medication, perhaps even seeing a psychiatrist. If you are in a situation where you are physically or mentally abused, achieving safety probably means getting out, finding a safe house. If you are in a situation where you are being harmed or potentially harmed in another way — a threat on the job, an impending divorce, a physical problem — it may mean getting yourself to the people or organizations that can support you.

There is a lot of help out there. Only when you need it during a crisis do we actually seek these resources.

Remember to Take Care of Business

The single most courageous act that anyone can perform is to take care of the day-to-day, moment-to-moment, sometimes-monotonous tasks of living. Taking care of business requires discipline, consistency, delaying of pleasure, and having faith that it is all worthwhile. The amazing leaps of risk and passion reward us instantly. The small, faith-filled steps of daily maintenance of self, relationship, community, loving, and teaching take, at times, enormous discipline and generosity.

Life requires of each of us some basics. We can skip over them only by paying a tremendous price. A daily rhythm of joy and sacrifice must be maintained for life to be complete. Some of these things seem meaningless: keeping receipts, eating well, doing homework, brushing our teeth, being gracious to our neighbors, exercising.

The simple act of performing these rituals, day after day, decade after decade, provides the pulse of our lives. When you honor this pulse, a crisis may shake you, but you will not fall. You can find yourself in crisis for a time, but following this beat, you will take yourself to higher ground. Something so simple is the most difficult, challenging act of all. More significant than profound visions or realizations or striking moments of good fortune is the ability to elevate the mundane acts of existence to their proper place as the supreme acts of creation.

If all you can do in certain moments is to maintain this beat or rediscover it if your life has been so traumatized that it has been temporarily lost, you will persevere, and in persevering, you will emerge triumphant. This pulse will keep you from allowing bumps to become mountains and valleys to become vortices. You will deal with reality as it occurs, and those who fall in step with you will represent an appropriate and powerful community that will guide you into tomorrow.

Exercise: Reaching Out

Your first task is to make a list of all of the people, organizations, activities, behaviors, and strengths that you can rely on. If you are ill that may mean finding a doctor you can trust and a social worker to help you get the services you need. If you are in physical danger, take care of the body first. Find a shelter. Go to legal aid. Call a friend. Eat. Bathe. Move — even if only to walk around your apartment.

Then make a list of the people who love you and reach out to them. Isolation is the enemy of survival. Don't cut yourself off from the energy and resources that can help you in the dangerous process you are going through. Once you reach out to a few of the resources on your list, that list will grow. Contact breeds contact.

To Find Help from Others, Give Your Crisis a Label

Often you can identify your new group (and remember, you may only be passing through) by its label. Alcoholics Anonymous. Women going through divorce. The jobless. New parents. Empty nesters. People with cancer.

If you have a difficult transition label such as "women-who-are-no-longer-in-love-with-their-husbands-and-don't-know-what-to-do" or "people-whom-life-has-passed-by," your continual work on your goal will eventually lead to a label. You can also ask your friends to participate in this exercise with you. Misery does love company. Even I, who go into a cave as a first response to crisis, can be drawn out by a few close friends, for whom I don't have to brush my hair, who have seen me at my lows.

Some of the groups may seem like ones you will never leave, for example, people with chronic illnesses or people who have waited too long to have children. Believe it or not, this crisis is not permanent. Even when you are confronted with an illness or a loss, or with something that you think will define you always, you will change your focus once you learn to manage the crisis and are reborn into your new life.

৵

When you are in crisis, you are a stranger in a strange land. You don't know where your supports are; your old rituals and systems don't support change, and yet change is what you must respond to. As a child, you clearly needed mentors. There were your parents, teachers, doctors, even police officers if you got lost in the street. You chose certain mentors because they had a style or profession that you admired and hoped to emulate in yourself.

Well, you are a *child* in this transition, and you can choose who you are going to become when you "grow up" in this new life. You need to find someone who knows the terrain. This can take the form of a book, a person, a group, an organization, a family member, or an activity that moves you forward.

Community supports us when we are challenged. Community also allows us to appreciate our strength in offering that strength to others in need. The pulse of community is the extension of the day-to-day, and engaging in community brings our power, consciousness, and resources outward into the entire world. Through community we create tomorrow every day, as we share the strength that empowers our own individual creations of self.

When small children are in crisis, experts encourage us to give them sameness of people, place, and things, to anchor them fully in the power of their own being and in the security of familiar surroundings. In crisis, when our "adult" constructs fail, nourishment is needed by our original, essential, child self. The compassionate eyes and arms of those who love us, and the wisdom of those who have traveled our road before us, give meaning and support to our journey when we cannot find it within ourselves.

Last year my son went away for a week of skiing with his father. Before he left, he asked me to take care of a rat that he had saved, and milk-fed, from the jaws of his father's snake. I have three true and fundamental fears in life — cockroaches, rats, and abandonment — and I was none too happy to have a rat in the house.

Of course, for my son I said yes. My stipulation was that he leave enough food and water in the cage so I wouldn't have to look at or touch the rat. The creature arrived at our house. I had my son put it at the far end of the hallway, where I couldn't see it but I could hear that it was okay.

Later that evening I went out to a party. I arrived back home around midnight. As I was preparing for bed, I heard a sniffling in the hallway. It was clear from the sound that the rat was having trouble breathing. I went online knowing, blessedly, nothing about rats and "Googled" *rats.* I was alarmed to learn that the number-one killer of rats was respiratory infections.

I immediately woke up my veterinarian (who still makes midnight house calls) and asked her what to do. She informed me that rats were considered "exotics," which she did not treat.

So here I was, in the middle of the night, with a rat who couldn't breathe and who was my greatest terror yet my son's beloved pet. Reluctantly, I turned on the steam shower, put a little lavender oil on my hand, and sat in my steam shower holding the dreaded, sick rat for most of the night. By morning, we were in love.

All I knew about rats was that a lot of them live on the streets of New York. I now wanted to learn everything about how to be a good rat parent. Online I found information about how to feed, breed, and communicate with rats, as well as rat language, rat humor, even rat chat lines. There was a whole rat-centered world that I was now a part of. Who would have thunk it?

So if you think that there is not a world to help you move through your transition, remember this rat's tale.

Once you have a label, you can find communities and resources from people who have successfully traveled the "country" before you. A wealth of information and actual help awaits you out there for anything you are going through. It is so important to be grounded in a community in order to navigate change successfully. A friend of mine has a favorite saying: "You don't know what you don't know" — and you don't. Luckily, others do.

People who have the money tend to pay experts to guide them through situations. This reliance is not always the best course of action. An expert has a particular point of view based on his or her experience. A community has a variety of experiences to share, and you can find a path within it that resonates for you. Often services and groups are available at local hospitals, social services, legal aid, and a variety of other common organizations.

Still, years after 9/11 — I live mere blocks from the former "ground zero" — our local hospital provides counseling, chiropractic adjustments, massage, and a host of other services free of charge to local residents. If you have computer access, go online and search for groups and organizations that can help the new you. There may be charities, newsletters, chat lines, government organizations, and more to give you the information and support you need.

Most important: remember that you are mastering your ability to choose who you are and where you belong. Your label will change, and as you move toward the re-creation of yourself, you will most often be the one who creates change instead of changes happening to you.

FIND WAYS TO TREAT YOURSELF

Expect Missteps, Faux Pas, and Other
Embarrassments — So Give Yourself a Break

I t astonishes me how much people fear making fools
of themselves and being at a loss for the right thing
to do, especially in new situations, and all the more
so considering the fact that all of us step on our own
feet (or someone else's) continually. Inelegance is something to *aspire* to when entering a new life. Trying some-

thing new, for which you have not yet acquired skills, takes courage. Wear the pie on your face as a badge of honor!

Consider Marta's story.

Marta was a single mother and a respected professional. She was always perfectly dressed, as were her eight-year-old twin daughters. Marta's kids had the fancy bag lunches on field trips and the best parties. One year, Marta realized that she was not going to make ends meet with rent, private school for the girls, childcare, and everything else that she had to handle on her own.

For a few months she kept up the image, while secretly panicking about what she was going to do. She let nobody know she was in trouble. Her weight dropped. She stopped seeing her friends. She planned more "alone time" with the girls since they could no longer afford the expensive weekend activities they had once enjoyed with their classmates. Marta felt like a complete failure. Even worse, she had failed her children. She was ashamed.

The December school bill went unpaid. The school sent another bill to remind her to pay the next semester.

One day when she went to pick up her daughters, a luxury she had gained from the drop in demand for her services, the head of the school walked over to her and started chatting. On impulse — impulse being something Marta had rarely felt, let alone acted upon — she told the head of the school that she was in a financial pit and would probably have to take her kids out of the school.

The headmistress looked her straight in the eye and said, "This is their school. They are not going anywhere." Marta received enrollment forms for the following year with all of the payment information canceled out. This experience made her feel braver about dropping the "person" that she had always been and leveling with people around her. She stopped wearing her lovely suits to pick up the kids and let herself be comfortable in jeans. She went out for coffee "with the ladies" after drop-off and let them know, in her unemotional, deadpan manner, that her "gilding" had worn thin.

Fast forward. Everyone loved the new, available, almost-relaxed Marta. And they finally felt like they had something to offer her. She got vacation invitations for the summer, "extra" days of housekeeping from a parent who had too much help, and most important, a posse of women finding her new clients.

By fall, she was back on her feet and able to pay tuition. She chose to be vigilant about not returning to the work-obsessed, perfection-obsessed person who had lost her gilding and gained a self.

❧

It is helpful to know what impressions you want to make in the new situations that you are confronting. How do you want to feel about yourself? How do you want others to respond to you? Simply posing these questions to yourself will help your intuition, intelligence, and awareness to guide you in being the person you want to be at any given time.

❧

That said, the surprises often teach us whom we are becoming. I am shy, somewhat uptight, and a tad controlling. When I first had to go public and do television interviews, I was terrified. It didn't help that I was also entering a child-custody battle and that everything I said could be used against me in court. I decided ahead of time that I needed to feel organized, sound rational (intuitives are so typecast), look put together (for court), and be seen as a serious, normal woman (court again). I did a few shows successfully (boringly) like that.

Then I was booked on the nationally syndicated morning show *The View*. I tried to be my "public person," but it just wasn't working. I felt like I was failing and worse, just my luck, on national television.

Frustrated, I decided just to go with the flow. I ended up joking, laughing, chatting with the audience and giving one of my best interviews ever. I wanted to feel competent to give something of real value to the audience. I ended up feeling warm, genuine, and entertaining, while providing the audience an accessible view of intuition.

I met a new me that day, the self that a minor crisis had brought forth. From that day forward, I enjoyed being interviewed. You will surprise yourself with the new people who emerge from inside you, and will find new joys in life as this process continues.

Accept the inevitable surprises as valuable lessons and

notice what you did and felt that was different from what you hoped or from your past experiences. This will allow you to more quickly evolve into the you who can thrive in your new incarnation.

Save Up Emotional Currency

While making sure you bank sufficient emotional and other reserves, don't deprive yourself of little pleasures. Even small, seemingly unimportant sacrifices in your well-being during crisis may prevent you from emerging from confusion and into clarity.

৯৹

We all know people who lose or gain tremendous amounts of weight when things go wrong in their lives. Then there are those people who chase pleasure, even destructive pleasure, when things go wrong. There are those who stop doing anything relaxing and pleasurable under stress. What do all of these people have in common, other than their stress? Their ability to manage the sensory needs and impulses has gone awry.

A sensory bank account promotes well-being. An appropriate balance of input and output creates strength. What are deposits to your sensory bank account? Anything that nourishes and delights your five senses without causing you harm in either the amount you are doing them or what you are doing.

When you overfeed one sense, you are usually starving another. Many overeaters have little awareness of the texture, flavor, sight, and smell of what they eat. People who overconsume alcohol numb their senses and sensibilities in an effort to feel less pain.

How do you remedy this? Especially during crisis, it is important to make sure that all of your senses are being fed and exercised regularly. Remember also that you have a sixth sense that needs feeding: your ability to perceive your environment through thought and memory. Cultivate nourishing thoughts. Search for positive memories that do not cause you nostalgia or other pain.

Exercise: Using a Memory

Right now, take a deep breath and allow yourself to be carried back to a comforting memory. You don't have to search for this memory, it will come to you; the choice will be made perfectly by your intuition, which will choose a memory to heal you and guide you even if you don't understand why or how it was chosen. Allow the memory to fill you as every sense, every thought, every muscle melts into this memory of comfort.

Allow this memory to transport you as it triggers another memory — the experience of comfort blending from one memory to the next, from one sense, sound, feeling, thought, taste, smell to another.

As you breathe the soft smell of comfort, allow yourself to notice the memories your intuition has chosen. What do they have in common? What elements, feelings, places, or situations in these memories are available to you *now?* Pick some elements in these memories that are available to you in your life now: a special park, a smell, a color, a person. Make a commitment to yourself to connect with that element of comfort in some way in your life. Allow the nourishment of comfort to remain with you as you open your eyes, seeking something in the room to notice that will bring you comfort.

ॐ

One way to ensure that you provide yourself with physical, emotional, spiritual, and other sustenance is to create rituals. Ceremonies — most especially, ones of celebration and mourning — are important concepts in daily life. Rituals mark progress, signal support for loss, and allow our inner as well as outer community to provide wisdom and support.

Make bedtime a moment of peace. Find an inspirational tape to speak over your own inner voice if you are having destructive "headspeak." Perform a small ritual that assures you that things are being resolved as you sleep. Go to sleep knowing the first positive act you will take the next morning. Make a list of things for your subconscious to work on or resolve in your sleep.

Take Time to Transcend the
Mundane Realities of Life

Transcendence. n 1: a state of being or existence above and beyond the limits of material experience 2: the state of excelling or surpassing or going beyond usual limits

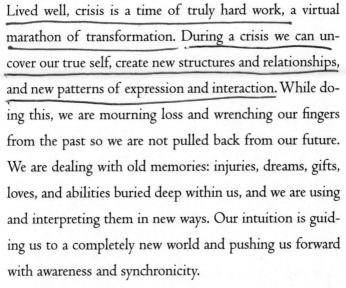

Lived well, crisis is a time of truly hard work, a virtual marathon of transformation. During a crisis we can uncover our true self, create new structures and relationships, and new patterns of expression and interaction. While doing this, we are mourning loss and wrenching our fingers from the past so we are not pulled back from our future. We are dealing with old memories: injuries, dreams, gifts, loves, and abilities buried deep within us, and we are using and interpreting them in new ways. Our intuition is guiding us to a completely new world and pushing us forward with awareness and synchronicity.

Although this process can be energizing and inspiring, it is always exhausting, frightening, and alien. In short, you need to recharge, to find your way back to your primal source of strength and support. You need to find experiences that transcend the "earth reality" of the moment and connect you to the wisdom and oneness that we all share and that offers you support and peace.

⁂

Even in battle, there are moments of peace. Those moments allow us to organize, energize, and synchronize ourselves with our core and with the world we love despite the situation we're in.

Each of us finds these pure moments in a different way. When my son, the extrovert, feels overwhelmed and needs peace and perspective, he throws himself into social interaction, losing himself in the oneness of camaraderie and community.

For me, the introvert, this release would be almost intolerable. I can interact only when I have energy to give; otherwise, it is a Herculean effort. I find my moments of transcendence in quiet and prayer, in listening to the voice of the universe whisper in the silence of my being.

My boyfriend recharges through experiencing the ideas of others but not necessarily in the company of others, losing himself in the information network of the Web, playing speed chess on the Internet, or reading books. It takes him out of himself and his experience and transports him to a place of nourishment and peace.

৵

Each of us recharges in his or her own way. Some of the ways people recharge include the following:

- meditation and prayer
- dancing and singing
- interacting with a group of people
- jogging
- researching new ideas
- eating wonderful food in wonderful company
- giving or receiving healing energy
- giving or receiving intuitive readings
- listening to another person
- being held
- taking part in a group ritual such as religious service or a celebration or even a funeral

- doing housework (yes, some people meditate this way)
- writing poetry and creating art

To use my language of transcendence: we all pray in different ways, but we all must pray.

Moments of transcendence remind you that you are an important part of something greater than yourself, something that can nourish, inform, transform, and carry you to a place of peace even when there is no peace in your material experience to be found. Transcendence takes you beyond the usual limits of self to where you can experience understanding from a new perspective and healing from allowing the energy of unity to carry you for a time.

These moments of unconscious experience provide the porous place where intuition and healing can slip in. Just as in sleep, when your muscles relax and receive nourishment, and your conscious mind takes a rest to download its circuits, organizing thought and feeling, moments of transcendence allow this process to occur in our daily waking life.

Seek these moments out. They are preserving and necessary. Children in natural periods of rapid growth need extraordinary amounts of sleep in order to grow properly. During a crisis, you need to cultivate moments of transcendence in order to move forward to your next level of being with strength, knowledge, perspective, and integrity. Transcendence allows you to rise above "earth reality" and rest the spirit and the senses from their awareness of struggle and conflict.

ஃ

One of the unique benefits of crisis is that once you commit to your crisis, you commit to its resolution. You cannot commit yourself to the past and move forward, and you cannot commit yourself to the future and have the attention and energy left over to deal with the present. Once you commit to being who you are in this moment, a wealth of tools and perceptions is available for your use.

- If you are an anger type, moments of transcendence may feel threatening, and you may avoid them in order to maintain the intensity of your rages. Not to do this feels unsafe to you. You will be far more powerful in your decisions and actions and far more convincing in your point of view with the perspective gained through moments of transcendence.

* If you are an anxiety type, you may avoid moments of transcendence because you feel that if you take your eye off the problem, it will overwhelm you. You cannot take action in every moment. If you give yourself a rest, not only will the problem become clearer, but also the solution will have a chance to find a place in your thoughts.

* If you are a depression type, you may avoid moments of transcendence because they require you to shift, even slightly, out of your secure pit, and this takes a bit of energy. Consider, however, that moments of transcendence will give you the support to make each of the required tasks of living easier.

* If you are a denial type, you may avoid moments of transcendence to keep your activity level high and avoid the revelation of that which scares, saddens, or angers you. Consider, however, that the moments of transcendence carry with them the wisdom and tools to resolve that which ultimately must be addressed for beauty and joy to be achieved.

❧

Life involves the struggle to integrate the often-divergent parts of self and the sometimes-antagonistic world around us. Life is the part that takes will, courage, determination, and heart. Transcendence is the gift from the bigger, but less defined, part of us that lets us know that what we are experiencing and achieving in our struggle to be human matters.

Our moments of transcendence give us the strength and understanding to continue on our journey with courage and direction. If you are not noticing your moments of transcendence, then you are missing the intermission part of the program. Moments of transcendence can be structured by practices such as meditating, being intentionally grateful, praying, giving and receiving healing, doing art, writing, playing with a child or a friend. Anything that allows your consciousness to take a rest while your body and subconscious are safe allows the freedom for the other part of you to connect once again to the whole from which it came and absorb the strength and knowledge that resides there.

Fortunately for us transcendence also comes when we are not safe. In crisis, when we are shaken and shifting, we are given life-saving, self-saving moments of clarity and direction.

෬

You grow through taking the next breath. You grow through pain, joy, and everything else. Yes, you would rather grow through joy, but you are where you are, and right now you are here, wherever that may be.

With transcendence, you leave your type behind. You are not reacting; you simply are. The wisdom of transcendent moments can be carried into your life through acts based on a new understanding. You will have the space and support to entertain a new model of reality.

- For the anxiety type, this is the assurance that you will get more chances, that few mistakes are terminal, and that you will find what you need in the world as well as within yourself.
- For the rage type, this means that you can have the opportunity to get, to do, and to have anything of

value that you missed. You can become everything that you could have become.

- For the denial type, this means that everything ultimately is all right, even without your denial. Clarity will not show you how you have been injured but how much you really do have.

- For the depression type, this means there is always enough support. You don't have to find the energy to do it alone. You are not alone. There is a place of peace, and it resides in you. The pain will ease; you can hand it over to a greater whole.

When transcendence is working in your life to recharge you, you may paradoxically need to revisit your own personal version of hell every so often just to say hello and experience how it and you have changed. As you gain the perspective and strength that transcendence provides, your old self and old world will call you back until you have made a complete transition.

The important discipline to remember in these moments is the practice of moderation. If you must rage, fear, hide, or sink, allow such explosions only for short and scheduled times. In my home we have adopted periodic "mental-health days": days when we just let it all go and un-ravel a bit. When practical — not when compelled — have a mental-health afternoon. Those times when you fall into unwanted states or behaviors without intending to, use your prescriptions religiously to regain your bearings and keep you on the path to the future of your desire and creation.

No New Damage

Doctors take the Hippocratic oath, the cardinal principle of which is the injunction "First, do no harm." Since we are the primary caretakers of ourselves, we would do well to follow this precept in our own lives.

∞

I want to share a profound concept introduced to me by Dr. Frank Miller, a prominent psychiatrist: no new damage!

In times of change and, frankly, in life in general, you are coping with so much every day just to take care of what is already on your plate that it is important to be vigilant about not creating anything new to deal with or placing yourself in situations likely to create additional difficulty.

Notice the people in your life who cause you trouble or make you feel less than you are. With every situation, interaction, and even opportunity, ask yourself, "What is the potential here for new damage?"

An innocent lunch date with a jealous childhood friend is an occasion for new damage. Not eating your breakfast if you are underweight is an occasion for new damage. Going to a mall and trusting yourself not to spend money that you don't have is an occasion for new damage.

Repeat after me: no new damage!

When toxic waste leaks into the environment, the damage done to the inhabitants in the area is directly related to their proximity to the disaster and the length of exposure. The same is true of hurtful people and situations from your past. The longer and closer your exposure to either, the more toxic you become.

Toxicity is antithetical to health. Health — the full use of your power for positive change — is your priority. For one day, keep a list of all the new damage you avoid now that you practice the law of "no new damage." You'll be amazed by the number of occasions for injury that occur each day.

≈

In crisis, we sometimes give ourselves permission to "let things slide." If ever there were a time when we can*not* afford that luxury, it is when we are coping with crisis!

It is not okay to make a mess; and if you do, you must clean it up. There was a reason that when we stole gum from Mr. Johnson's candy store, our mothers made us go back and confess. If you make a mess, clean it up — especially when you are in a crisis.

≈

Here's what you've already achieved in this chapter:

- You have begun the process of creating a community that reflects back to you a new and masterful way of being in your new world.

◆ You are opening your life up to every kind of support that will give you the knowledge, strength, and inspiration to conclude this crisis successfully.

◆ You are finding a new and unique expression of yourself, a voice in your world and in yourself being heard and acknowledged by others in constructive and transformative ways.

◆ You are engaging intuition and unity to guide you through effective change.

◆ You have earned your badge of courage by putting one foot in front of the other and advancing into the unknown.

Mourn Your Loss and Honor the End

Loss is the part of life that insists that you build a more authentic self and a more authentic life. Things fall apart. If you could have successfully clung to your life at the age of five, or ten, or fifteen, who would you be now? Remember this when you are tempted to reach back to what is no longer there. You will make a new life. You are making it now.

Take a moment to make a list of the ways in which both you and the possibilities in your life might be improved by this crisis. If you cannot think of positive possibilities right now, *make things up*.

For example, "My marriage collapsed."

- I am learning to love myself.
- I am meeting new people.
- Everyone is being nice to me.
- Doors are opening for me.
- I am going to demand a good relationship next time.
- I have a better relationship with my family.
- I am being offered lots of opportunities for new experiences from concerned friends.
- I finally lost that extra ten pounds on the misery diet.
- I am finding my sense of humor.

Of course, at the end of the list, your response will probably be, "Who gives a damn?" These things are important to be aware of, however, so you can strengthen and quicken the process of change by "tempting" yourself toward forward movement. One day, I guarantee, you will give a damn again.

Ask your friends, maybe your therapist, to help. Even the most horrific set of facts can create a stronger, more able, happier you. The first step is to redirect your attention to how the crisis is making you confront a new world and a new you and then finding aspects of these changes to appreciate.

I know how ludicrous this suggestion might sound. Celebrating the aftermath of a crisis does not make it all okay. It is, however, the only way to make you okay within it. You need to survive the crisis and find ways that the changed you can grow from the experience.

The alternative is to remain damaged, and this option is not acceptable for you or your life. In order to avoid remaining damaged, you could do the following:

- Have a job-search brunch.
- Start a journal just for recording the successes of your new life.
- Ask your friends to designate a day on which everyone spoils you.

- Dress the new you (if you are strapped for cash, secondhand from friends or your own closet works fine).

- Hang around people who celebrate the person you are becoming.

- Ask friends to make a day to prepare you for your new reality.

- Ask all of your friends to e-mail you what they like best about how you've changed. (You can phrase it in a funny way so this feels less embarrassing. "I feel like a belly crawler. I am trying to find good in this experience. Any observations about how it has changed me for the better would be greatly appreciated.")

The possibilities are endless.

≫

If what you lost, whatever it was, didn't have value to you, you wouldn't be in crisis now. When a loss occurs we continue the unfinished business of mourning all the losses that we have experienced in our lifetime. We are never capable of digesting an experience completely, and every reminder or even reinjury gives us the opportunity to continue the process of healing our past.

When someone dies, his or her bereaved friends and family need to grieve. Yet the first thing the loved ones do is not mourn — but rather, take care of business. Bringing family together. Wrapping up loose ends. Finding out about insurance. Arranging for the burial. Handling the estate.

Mourning comes only after the business of the moment has been taken care of, although the loss is felt simultaneously. When business isn't taken care of, when the new and ongoing demands of life are ignored, families get into trouble.

Amazingly, in taking care of the business of your new life, you are already easing your transition into your new life. Even without understanding how, simply changing your behavior is often enough to catalyze a cascade of positive changes in your life. In changing your behavior, you automatically begin to deal with the crisis or upheaval.

In doing the exercises in this chapter you have made it safe to take a moment to mourn this loss and every other loss that came before it. Write a poem. Light a memorial candle. Sing a sad song and cry. Talk to the old you for a moment, the one who believed in what is no longer. It is okay to be sad. Grief is a necessary element of change. When you experience grief without either falling into it or defending against feeling it, you acknowledge the importance of what came before where you are and who you are now. Structure times to grieve and to ask for and receive comfort from yourself and from others.

My mother's birthday and her "death day" are both in March. Those two days border my birthday, which I share with my son, and my boyfriend's birthday, which precedes ours by a day. I dedicate each March to celebration and mourning, mourning and celebration, and then I move into April renewed.

Avoiding the Three Death Traps: Rumination, Recrimination, and Retribution

In this chapter I am asking you to relinquish three seductive mental habits: rumination, recrimination, and retribution. I refer to these habits as death traps because they keep you tethered to a life that no longer exists. These death traps are seductive because they provide the illusion of hope. Rumination allows you to relive the past over and over, replaying different endings and permutations to the same old haunting scenarios. Recrimination helps keep loss at a distance by shifting your attention and blame to someone or something you hold responsible.

Retribution allows you to maintain the fantasy that whoever or whatever injured you will have to make you whole.

Rumination, recrimination, and retribution, however, divert your attention from where it should be — on improving your life now and in the future — and keep it rooted in the past. You and I are going to say good-bye to these three dangerous black holes for your attention and emotional energy.

Forgetfulness-Forgiveness-Faith-Fullness

Before we travel through the painful territory of the three R's — rumination, recrimination, and retribution — let's conduct an experiment in healing.

Take a moment to entertain the notion that you can forget your crisis and forgive the people, incidents, or forces of nature that injured you in the first place. Pretend that the universe — God, your inner wisdom, wherever your faith lies — supports you and that you have enough, right now, for your own happiness and healing. Imagine how you would be in this moment if this were true.

We reexperience our losses many times before we are done. Each time we revisit a loss, the experience is different because we are different; we have gained something from our past encounters. Grief should not be a place we inhabit, even in the most difficult periods of our lives. Grief should be a place that we visit while performing the essential, sustaining activities of life. Periods of mourning serve a purpose, but sometimes they are artificially brief.

No matter which response type you are (chapter 4), there are three R's that affect everyone during crisis: recrimination, rumination, retribution. Once you move to a different place in the alphabet, you have the full use of your energy, focus, and resources for the present and the future. The three R's tie you firmly, toxically, to the past.

Understanding Recrimination

Let's first look at recrimination and its healer, forgiveness. Certain things should never be tolerated, physical and emotional abuse among them. For the victim to survive, however, the energy needs to be removed from what has happened to what is happening right now. The ability to survive is what the victim needs to become the victor.

Forgiveness is not — you denial types — pretending something never happened. Nor — you anger types — is it a vendetta. Why waste energy on someone who has injured you? It is not — you anxiety types — accepting damage. You are not damaged unless you choose to be. You can use all experience to take you where you want to go. And it is not — you depression types — taking the blame on yourself or accepting the injury as your problem.

Forgiveness is born from the realization that you can heal the past only in the present. Forgiveness is choosing to take your energy and resources and redirect them to the present and your current objectives. When you hold on to blame, whether you are blaming yourself or another, you hold on to damage. Forgiveness is the act of giving the present your full attention. When you forgive, you refuse to allow another person or situation to hold your power. Forgiveness is making yourself more important than anything that was done to you.

Of course, you are the hardest person to forgive. Even when you are clearly the victim, there is always an element of self-blame for making yourself vulnerable in the first place. Neither blame nor guilt is useful or rational. Neither blame nor guilt helps you move forward in your life. It is our misguided attempt to revise the past by staying in the past. We have the illusion of power: the power of right, the power of our emotion. If we let the guilt and blame go, we are left to confront the damage. That, however, is exactly what we must do.

 You forgive not because it is the right thing to do, but because it is the only way the old situation will not occupy the space in your life that your new body-job-relationship-life should fill. No matter how empty life may feel at times, life is always full. There is no space for truly new and authentic people and experiences in your life if you do not let go of the old. This knowledge alone is often enough to help you with the difficult process of forgiveness.

Every time that you are finding it difficult to forgive, notice the place in your life that the old situation or person is occupying. Are you willing to give up something wonderful, authentic, and real for that connection to the past? For example, anger at your father may be filling the space that would otherwise be occupied with good, supportive people who believe in you and support you the way he should have. Blaming your sister for her bad behavior is filling the space that could be filled with understanding. If you can't forgive your ex, your primary relationship is with your ex. Who wants that? Why not try someone new who could and would want to fill your needs? If you can't forgive life, God, your employer, and so on, you cut off your ability to make an authentic change.

When you forgive you are not excusing the injurious behavior, person, or event. You are simply refusing to allow it to occupy a space in your life. Human beings are hard-wired to survive and thrive. If you maintain the awareness that when you withhold forgiveness you lose, forgiveness becomes your pattern. You will not find the knife in your back again just because you have forgiven. You will have taken the growth from the experience without perpetuating the damage.

To forgive, you need to acknowledge to yourself what you feel that you've lost and acknowledge that holding on to those feelings merely perpetuates the sense of loss. Forgiveness releases the sense of loss and frees up the energy that had been trapped by recrimination. Forgiveness liberates and empowers you. To help you realize the emotional and psychic costs of recrimination, you may want to write down the other uses to which you could devote your otherwise wasted energy.

Here are some examples:

- ◆ I acknowledge that the world let me down. I got a great college degree and looked for a job, and I still am unemployed. I forgive the situation, and I choose to use the energy I free to attract the perfect job to me and allow myself to make the shifts that make this possible.

Or:

- ◆ I forgive my father. I take back the power he had to make me feel small, and I use this power to empower myself.

Or:

- ◆ I forgive my employer for firing me, and I choose to use this energy to attract the job that I really want.

Or:

- I forgive myself for letting myself be fooled and hurt by a partner once again, and I choose to use this energy to love myself so only people who wish me well can reach me.

Or:

- I forgive God (or the universe or the God within) for taking this loved one from me. I am going to reclaim this energy so I can love again.

Remember the old saying "forgive and forget." In order to let go, you need to forgive. You need those hands to build, comfort, love, create, and master a new, wonderful life. If you do not forgive, you keep yourself anchored to a past that no longer serves you.

Understanding Rumination

It is natural to want to go back and change how something happened, what you said, how you felt or made another feel. Rumination, however, is the impotent longing for healing.

Rumination is my personal favorite costly indulgence: the mind voyage of woulda, shoulda, coulda, what if, and if only. Rumination is the act of constant fantasy, time travel to revisions and outcomes that can never be. Rumination is self-injury. You take your energy from the present and keep it in a place where you have no power, the mulling over of the past. You are the director of your own movie, which no one will ever see. Rumination is a popular way we avoid dealing with the real, visceral, energy-consuming unpleasantness of the present. Rumination keeps you in a familiar environment: your past, your fantasy, and the illusion of control that keeping life quarantined in your own head can give you.

Using a simple technique called telepathic dialog (page 179), you can change the dynamic of an event. This technique works for healing something in the past, the present, or even the future. Often you will find that the person or people you are dialoging with actually have a change of attitude or even contact you to continue the conversation that you had intuitively from a distance.

৯৹

I had a workshop student diagnosed with early-stage lung cancer. She had never smoked. She didn't work in a profession with environmental hazards. Her family had no history of cancer and, yet, here she was, with lung cancer.

When I saw her, all of her energy was directed toward finding a reason why this was happening. What did she do? What could she have changed? She had read a book that said that lung cancer was about unresolved grief. How could she have done this to herself? Was it because her mother had left the family? Was this her mother's fault? Had her mother stayed, would she now be healthy? Had she gone to therapy and resolved her grief, could she have avoided this crisis?

All her energy was going to these thoughts. Here was what she did not have the focus and energy to do: She did not schedule the surgery that, though unpleasant, stood a good chance of saving her life. She did not look into alternative therapies to address the problem. She did not find a community to guide her through the process. She did not address the structures of her life in a way that would make the process of healing as smooth as possible. All of the things that could have made the crisis a short, unpleasant episode were sacrificed to her ruminations.

She came to the workshop to be healed. Her partner did a laying on of hands, also known as a psychic healing. After the healing, the student asked her partner, "Do you think I am healed?" Her partner didn't have an answer and was so upset that it became a class discussion. We urged her to deal with the "earth reality," the nuts and bolts of her situation. We advised her to get information and attempt everything possible — healing, therapy, surgery, support — to give herself the best chance of healing in a way that would make her life the kind of life she wanted. We suggested to her that not dealing with the anger and grief that this situation brought up might be the reason why she had never had a long-term relationship or committed herself to a satisfying career. We pointed out the opportunity available in dealing with these issues, having surgery before the cancer progressed, and moving forward into a life that she had always wanted but been unable to create for herself. People offered to do research for her, to be a voice on the other end of the phone. A lovely elderly woman even offered to stay with her after surgery to mother her. The student thanked them for their support and then asked, "Do you think I am healed?"

I wish I could give you an uplifting postscript to this story. I never heard from or saw her again. I have a policy of not following up on people unless they ask me to. My hope is that she received enough support and guidance from the workshop to take immediate and appropriate action, but I doubt that was the case. My best guess is that she stayed in her thoughts until the cancer had progressed to the point that she was in real and urgent pain, the kind of pain that forces you into the present. Sadly, by that time her prognosis would probably not have been good.

Dealing with rumination requires discipline. There is some comfort in going back to a place we know, even a painful place. It allows us not to deal with a present that we feel challenged by and a future that is foreign. You can and must deal with the pull toward the past by consciously focusing your energy on the present. This focus needs to be active and detailed. Every time you find yourself slipping into rumination, find one thing to do — make coffee, pay a bill, take a shower, anything — to put you in present time. Direct the soothing quality of fantasy not at the past but toward the future. Make fantasies that exclude the past but that are hopeful, comforting, and motivating. The following are some activities that will help you do this:

- Draw a picture of your wish come true. When you are done, examine the picture and record your impressions. You will give yourself so much useful information from your subconscious and your intuition using this technique. You may even want to show this picture to a friend and ask what he or she notices about it. Allow yourself and your life, as you are right now, to be interesting and compelling to you.

- Talk to yourself a year from now. Really be yourself a year from this very day. Pretend that life has worked out just fine, although your past is behind you (can't have your wife come back; can be in a really loving, passionate, committed relationship) and let your future self tell your present self how you are doing, with lots of juicy details. I love to put this down on paper, like a script, but you can just close your eyes and do it verbally.

- When you need to visit the past, do it for only a short and structured time.
- Students in my workshop have had very interesting experiences with an exercise that we do in pairs, with one person becoming the person or situation that the other person wants to talk to. Often students will pick someone whom they haven't heard from in a long time or can't seem to have a conversation with without fighting. Frequently within a few weeks the person will actually call them to resume the dialog that they started (unbeknownst to them) in the telepathic dialog (page 179).

Rumination takes you back to a place that no longer exists and cannot be re-created. You can heal the past only in the present. It is here that your power, inspiration, and healing can work miracles and rectify the wrongs of the past.

Understanding Retribution

The seeds of retribution are the seeds of healing. They are the desire to be made whole by the act of a just outcome. The fantasy of repayment for injury and the compensation for loss allows us to feel powerful and whole again. I have seen people hold out for retribution from a spouse or employer who wronged them. I've also seen people refuse to build anything good in life as a demand for retribution against a God or universe they feel betrayed them. Crisis is often accompanied by indigestible injustices, and they are just that, indigestible. At some point you and your survival, success, and happiness have to be more important than who or what did you wrong. The farther you take yourself from both the injustices in life and the unjust, the more power you will have to create what is truly meaningful to you.

That said, I am not speaking of the injustices that many of us address as our obligation to helping others. These have a reason for us beyond the effort to make ourselves whole. I am speaking of those deeply personal, rarely winnable battles to reclaim a piece of ourselves from a situation where we were harmed. The reality is, as Italians say, *"Vendetta e un piatto che va mangiato freddo"* (Revenge is a dish best eaten cold). In other words when you are suffering in the heat of feeling injured, you are capable of harming only *yourself.*

You are ineffective in obtaining retribution. Only when reason returns can you use your resources effectively to cause harm, although with distance and perspective, it is rarely how you will choose to spend your energy. The simple way to convince yourself out of retribution is to allow yourself to be aware of the reality that you will cause yourself far more harm than you will inflict on another when you seek retribution in the heat of the moment. Leave retribution for a time when you are calm, powerful, and objective, and then if you care to, you will exact your revenge.

What is more effective is to acknowledge that you are angry and that you need to feel powerful again and then do the things that will help you metabolize anger (see the prescriptions for the anger type) and take effective action, however small, to build your new life.

Here are some things that you can do when overwhelmed with the desire for retribution.

- Examine your retribution fantasy. Ask yourself what you would be getting from it other than the satisfaction of seeing the other person pay. Know that if you are waiting for the other person to give this to you, it will not only be a long wait, but you will also not be actively getting this for yourself another way. In other words you are leaving the power with them to keep yourself from getting your needs met. Now focus all of that hot, angry energy on pretending that they don't exist and getting your needs met another way. Make a list of how that could happen.

+ Have a funeral ritual. Invite some close friends over and bury the person or situation (metaphorically, of course — oh if only), in all of his or her wickedness. Say a eulogy, speak as long as you like, let the things that come out of your mouth surprise you. Take a few minutes to mourn the loss, speak about the person you have now become (in positive terms, as if you had already achieved your goal), and have a little party. I have done this ritual, which I call a funeral and a wedding, countless times in my workshops. It is satisfying, cathartic, and healing.

+ Put a pillow in front of you and let the pillow be the person or situation you want to exact revenge on. Yell at the person. Tell him or her what you think and that you are taking your power back. Let the person know what you are becoming (keep it positive, please) and that he or she failed in the effort to disempower you. Do this until you cry, laugh, or have some other releasing emotional expression that soothes you.

- Make a list of things that the person or situation has taken from you. In your imagination see (or if you don't visualize things, simply feel or experience in any other way) the person in front of you, and one by one reach out and take these things back, letting him or her know that these things belong to you and that he or she may no longer possess them.
- You can do these remedies whenever your attention goes to retribution.
- When you take your energy back, it is interesting how others respond. We are connected energetically to the people and experiences in our past. When you dissolve the connection and take back what is yours, the magic in your life begins, and you remove your magic and power from the person who harmed you.
- "Living well is the best revenge." Now there's a healing homily.

Rumination, recrimination, and retribution are all ways that you keep yourself rooted in the familiar past.

All loss involves a sense of betrayal. You may have betrayed yourself by allowing a bad situation to continue, giving up power that you are now paying for, maintaining a bad habit such as overeating or smoking that you now realize is stealing your life. You may have been betrayed by your own growth. You may no longer desire things, people, or situations that you thought you would treasure forever. You may have been betrayed by a person, your body (as with illness), your company, your society or community, or even your idea of God. The laws that you lived by have been changed, either through an event or through your awareness, and you trust them no longer.

When you are betrayed, you need to find a new source of power in the world, in your sense of self and in your beliefs. The place to start is with your interaction in the world, the details, the "earth reality" of your situation. It is the results from this new source of power that will give you real and concrete feedback that you can use to create your situation; you are not lost but rather temporarily misplaced. You can find new and more appropriate beliefs. You will find that you have not lost yourself but have become more of a self that can function creatively and powerfully in your new world. Most important, the world around you will respond to your actions in a new and empowering way.

This does not mean that everything around you magically falls into place. Learning how to walk means falling, getting back up, dusting yourself off, and having the determination to try again. Don't judge your efforts. The time and energy spent in judging yourself is better directed toward taking the step again. Failures are clues that success is at hand. They mean you are trying.

The depressed person, our thinker, will ask, "Why bother trying if you will only be betrayed again?" I'll tell you why: you have no choice. Some belief in the structures you work with is necessary for you to use them. Yes, some of these structures will ultimately betray you, as you will ultimately grow past some of them and betray your old self. Whoever said that in order to be trustworthy something had to be perfect was a denial type. Nothing is perfect unless you accept it as such.

"*Che si accontenta, gode*," say the Italians: "He who contents himself, enjoys." Betrayal is a part of the perfect imperfection of life. Take joy from what is simply, imperfectly acceptable to you. The anger types will say, "That's not fair, and I don't accept it." Not accepting what is available, and it is a lot, is simply biting off your nose to spite your face. Reality is not optional.

Your only choice is in determining how you want to live in the real world and create what you want. You anxious ones ask how to deal with the fear of imperfection. You need to deal with fear as its own animal. Imperfection, once integrated into your reality, is simply something to be factored into a fruitful and joyful existence.

How should we deal with betrayal? We recognize that it is a necessary part of growing into happiness, creativity, and fulfillment. We cannot stay the same and thrive. Nothing can. Not oceans, not people, not relationships, not companies, not societies.

The ultimate gift of betrayal is authenticity. As hard as this is to realize when you are betrayed, what you are left with is the beginning of who you really are: the faith in yourself that you can rely on your inner strength, intuition, judgment, and choice. You can be who you truly are in each stage of your life and growth and have your needs filled appropriately. Would you really still want to drink from a baby bottle or be carried everywhere or wear diapers? Yet the removal of all of these supports was viewed as a betrayal. What did you learn? You learned that you could administer your own needs and rewards.

Yes, I wish my mother had thought about the four children she was leaving behind when she committed suicide. I wish my critical, perfectionist father had helped me feel more valuable and special. I wish my husband had kept his financial promises. However, at the present moment I have friends and a family who mother me more than I can sometimes tolerate, I have plenty of things and people in my life who make me feel like the cat's meow (including my father), and I have a career that supports me just fine. I would not give up a single thing that I have created from these betrayals to have lived the original experience differently.

You will not get your needs met in the past. I can love my mother without longing, enjoy my father for what he has to offer and acknowledge how my relationship with him helped me attract a loving, affirming man into my life, and acknowledge that my financial need gave me one of the most treasured elements in my life, my career. Make yourself more important than the people and situations that you have left behind or that have left you.

As you move from reacting to creating, you are sure to become aware of what you have lost in a clear, specific, and realistic way. Once again, all change involves loss. Even if you've lost something you wanted to lose — weight, a bad habit, a bad job, a difficult partnership — that something *defined* you. Your new self is able to evaluate that something with increasing objectivity. Objectivity and reality can be painful, but this stark pair forms a solid base on which to build your dreams.

Ask yourself now what would make you feel like you have what you need. What would the picture of a healed you look like? Commit to that picture. Draw it, speak it, dance it, ask people to help you create it. Take time to embody that portrait, to pretend it already exists so intuition can help you find the resources to recognize it as it happens.

The hard thing about crisis is that you rarely get practice moving through it successfully. People tend to respond in type to crisis, as discussed in chapter 4. Anger people seethe and blow up. Depression people give up. Anxiety people either freeze altogether or engage in frenzied, irrational activity, while denial people ignore the problem until it grows to such mammoth proportions that it threatens to erode everything in their lives.

২৯

If you want to, play things over in your mind, work them out before the crisis. Companies that prepare for different futures use a technique called scenario planning.

Imagine the following scenario. You have just been fired from your job, left by your spouse, or diagnosed with an illness. How do you feel? What are you going to do? What is your immediate reaction? What do you know that your reaction should be? Take yourself through this crisis to its conclusion. Do it as quickly as possible. In a minute.

Now be methodical in the same crisis. Use what you have learned thus far in this book. What could you have done differently? What options are open to you? Who can help? What do you need to know about yourself to survive this crisis? How would the outcome have changed?

Practice crisis scenarios in which you survive and

thrive. Your intellect and intuition is engaged in learning solutions before problems arise.

☙

Scenario planning can even be made into a game. I played a game up until the birth of my son called the Time Travel Game. If I could go back in time knowing what I know now, what would I change?

Of course, in my early fantasies I would rescue my mother, save my grandmother's old fairy-tale books, confront the nasty headmistress of my primary school, and so on. I am now, however, far too practical and grounded to think that by changing the losses I would preserve something of value. What if I had rescued my mother and she had continued to try to commit suicide, which she surely would have, and I continued to expend all of my energy and time caring for her? What if I had confronted my headmistress and been kicked out of my comfortable private school?

And what if, when my son was born, I could no longer play this game? I wouldn't change a single detail about him. If I'd had a different life, he would be a different person.

There is nothing about him that changed I would not miss. That said, the single event that drew me into the longest crisis of my life where I was underarmed in every way was the birth of my son. Yet I look at him often and wonder how I ever lived in a world that did not have him in it. I would relive every painful moment in my past to be with him now.

Rumination Sometimes Disguises
Itself as Introspection

In the past century new disciplines such as psychology, psychiatry, and psychoanalysis have sprung up around the notion that only by understanding our problems or crises can we begin the healing process. I would like to propose the heretical notion that attempting to understand traumatic events should be postponed until the healing process is well under way, if not postponed indefinitely.

When major crises shake up our lives, it is natural to want to understand what caused these events. But in the rush and tumult of life, this effort to understand is largely a waste of time. In the first place, such understanding in "real time" is ultimately impossible; we need distance and perspective to understand the major events in our lives. Equally important, when you are handling a crisis, you need all of your mental, emotional, and other resources directed toward taking care of business.

What you would have, should have, could have done before will not help you in the moment, now. The life you are living may not have its foundation on the life you lost or on the resources of the life that you *will* have. What you can do now, understanding where you are now, and how to best use what you have now, are the pressing questions you need to spend your energy and ingenuity answering.

One of the biggest mistakes you can make in the face of radical change, then, is to postpone taking action until you can fully evaluate your situation and options. If you live in the moment, with the tools of the moment, you can move forward toward wholeness immediately. Ruminating about your past, reliving your "mistakes" and disappointments (invariably involving heavy doses of unhealthy self-recrimination) keeps you frozen in the past. Put your attention on what you can do *now*.

Don't get me wrong. Therapeutic counseling can play an important role in the healing process. To the extent that understanding a traumatic event is possible, however, such understanding will come only with the passing of time and with the gaining of distance and perspective.

In the meantime you must move forward in your life.

You Must Let Go of Pain, Too

Rumination, recrimination, and retribution keep us mired in pain. One of the things that keeps our selves from advancing is our attachment to pain. <u>To transform your life, you must find a way to cope with the pain of crisis, if not detach from that pain.</u>

෨

How many times has your life been ruined, over, shattered beyond recognition? Yet, here you are, whole enough to be reading these words.

෨

No pain, no gain, right? And what doesn't kill you makes you stronger. Or does it?

I hate the "pain-is-good-for-you" cliché.

Pain hurts. And chronic pain undermines our ability to survive, much less evolve.

۶۰

Yet we hold on to our pain. That's how we convince ourselves that we've let go — even when we're still holding on. Letting go of the pain means letting go of our connection to its source: our old life! In that moment the grieving truly begins. Pain injures; grief soothes.

۶۰

We are each of us and all of us here in this life to teach and to learn. But our lessons need not be as painful as they sometimes are.

We have a choice in the form our lessons take. When we live consciously we can say to the universe, "Teach me another way!"

۶۰

Consider the word *meaningful*. When you choose to make an experience meaningful, you become an observer in the situation. When an experience is made useful to us, it is also made bearable. We know how to contextualize and direct its impact.

In crisis, it is difficult to understand the meaning of what you are going through in the moment, but you can still direct your experience toward an understanding that will take you to a better place in your life. To do this, keep in mind your results of the type test and your reaction style.

 The value of even our losses makes sense once we understand that life is a continuum. We help each other throughout many lifetimes. Never, ever, think that you are alone, or that your struggles are meaningless. Our struggles are often painful — at times, extremely so — but never meaningless.

Truly we are here in this life to learn and to teach at the same time.

You may wonder how you can be a teacher to others when at times, such as in crisis, you struggle to accomplish the simplest tasks. The explanation is in our connectedness. When a tree is injured by insects, fires, or the elements, it secretes protective fluids. In itself that is not so remarkable. But scientists have discovered that when a tree on one side of a forest has been damaged — the trees on the *far* side of the forest also secrete protective fluids.

Like the trees, we are all connected — you, and I, and everyone else. And what you learn in your life, and through your struggles, *everyone* learns.

You are every person in crisis. Every seemingly unfair hit that fate throws your way affects us all. And when you survive your crisis, you teach us *all* how to survive it.

During crisis you will probably not have the same things to give to others that you used to. When I was married I had lots of money, and I could give money to friends and family members on a consistent basis.

During my crisis I no longer had money to give. This made me feel like I was just a pathetic needy person, and to be honest, some of my relationships didn't survive. The only thing I really had to give was my intuition and insight.

Intuition has always been a natural, comfortable part of me, so I felt as if I were giving very little.

Years later I found out that this was far more valuable a gift to many of my friends than my money had been. It was also a gift that connected me intimately to the lives of those I loved.

Let's take a moment together to mourn your loss and to acknowledge that the mourning will be revisited on and off until you have fully created your new life. When you no longer allow the three R's to keep you in the past, you may experience your loss more fully. The fear of this is what kept you attached to the loss in the first place.

Mourn, cry, ask people to mourn with you. Even if it was a bad job, marriage, habit, whatever it was, you have a right to miss it, mourn it, and have people honor the loss with you.

Know, although it hurts unbearably and you can't even imagine getting through this time in your life — you hurt so bad that you can't even imagine what relief would feel like — that pain can be fuel, and when you're using it as fuel, you won't experience it as pain.

Exercise: Telepathic Dialog

One of the reasons we stay stuck in the past with rumination, recrimination, and retribution is the feeling that we cannot go back and undo the past, especially when the people or situations in question have moved on. The telepathic-dialog technique discussed earlier can be adapted to countless other situations, but for now we will use it to help you resolve issues that cannot otherwise be resolved (for example, issues you might have with someone who is no longer in your life).

Take a long deep breath and notice all of your senses as well as your thoughts. Allow yourself to sense, in any way you are able, the other person with you. Take a moment to notice what this person (your subject) needs to feel, see, hear, or know to have healing with you. Notice what you need to feel, remember, see, or hear to convey that message to your subject. Send those feelings, impressions, memories, and sounds to your subject by feeling those sensations yourself and simultaneously feeling your subject feeling them.

Bring the person or situation to mind. Notice yourself and notice the person or situation as separate from you, your mind, so you can go back and forth between you and "it" in your mind's eye.

Give the image or situation that is in your mind's eye a sense of reality. For the moment allow yourself to act as if you truly can communicate with this person or situation.

It may even help to pick a spot on the wall and imagine the person there or put a cup on the table and imagine the person there. Remember, you won't necessarily *see* the person. You may simply feel his or her presence or otherwise "know" that the person is there.

Begin by asking, in your mind, what you need to know from this person — then wait for a response. Both the response and the question can involve using all of your senses. You can see, feel, hear, smell, taste, or just know what the question or answer is. After you do this for a few minutes, you will begin to feel a flow of information and sensation back and forth between you and your "imaginary" partner.

The idea is to resolve the situation to some degree. You need to discuss with this person what is going on and try to find ways to come to a good resolution. Wait for the person's response; don't invent it and try not even to anticipate it. You will sense the person's response in many different ways. You might well hear it, see it, feel it, or *sense* it in another way.

This exercise can be frustrating, as you are not relating to the person's "higher self," but rather to the person himself, with all of the weaknesses he and the situation have in real life.

You may need to repeat this exercise many times, and what you discover from this exercise may be that there is no resolution from working directly with the situation. In that case the objective is for you to express what you need to express until you feel some closure. Often you may find that the "imaginary" person spoken to calls a few days later to "continue" the conversation.

If you are comfortable writing, you may want to write this exercise as you do it, or at least begin the exercise that way. You can also use a tape recorder.

You must be absolutely clear about breaking the connection after the exercise is done. Also, do not attempt this exercise for more than five minutes at any one time; you do not want to become more enmeshed with this difficult person or situation unconsciously. The idea is to take some time to dialog consciously, connect and negotiate, and in doing so take the "dynamic" from inside yourself and move it to a place where the other person (or situation) is "outside" yourself, allowing you some perspective and clarity about who you are and what your options are.

One of the most amazing parts of this exercise is that the dialog often continues in real life, as if you had actually been able to negotiate and communicate during the exercise. Life is lived on so many levels. The more of them we train to a state of health, the more powerful we are to create change in a positive and powerful way.

REWRITING YOUR PERSONAL
MYTHOLOGY

So, *who are you?* Our recurring question that we encountered first in the opening of chapter I.

You are not your story. In fact your story is inaccurate, subjective, and — unless it is helping you achieve — superfluous. You are your choices. There are so many tales of people who were failures yet, when faced with crisis, built great things and, in the process, became great themselves. Alas, an equal number of stories feature high-school stars who failed later in life.

Your story does not dictate your life — *your choices do.*

✸

We all have a story, a drama, a myth that we act out repeatedly in our lifetimes. Usually it is an inherited story, created before we were even born by the story of our parents and the circumstances of our birth, most often given to them by the same formula. The world around us and the people in it are simply actors in this drama.

✸

What is your personal mythology? If you aren't sure, think about how your parents or siblings would have described you. I was the "responsible one" in my family. I have a sister who was the "identified patient." And then there was the "pretty one." Often you are still living the personal mythology given to you in childhood.

In moments of transition, your obsolete personal mythology is particularly dangerous to you. Consider Jeff's story.

Jeff always knew that he was special. Although he had a difficult childhood, he had an extraordinary talent that made people take notice and treat him differently. He had many early work successes as an adult. He was such a character that no one really noticed that he could never order something off the menu at a restaurant without making a handful of changes to the dish. At tax time, when everyone was running silly to get their returns in on time, he figured he would do it when it was convenient, which was never. If something was unpleasant, he just avoided it, "protecting" himself as if he were made of glass.

Then, when he was about thirty, he stalled. Work wasn't moving. He had never really had time for relationships. He was frequently "tired," and often irascible, sometimes given to temper outbursts. He hadn't gone to the doctor, dentist, accountant, or lawyer in years. He had relied on his "specialness" to keep him safe. At forty his life was a mess, but it never occurred to him to do the day-to-day, monotonous things that the rest of us mortals do to make it better. Someone took him to a therapist, but of course, he was smarter than the therapist and felt that the therapist couldn't understand him.

Jeff had no format for getting help. His personal mythology had brought him to a point of crisis. It hit him when his resources were so limited that he couldn't maintain the isolated, special nature of his lifestyle. By the time his crisis hit, his body, finances, career, and relationships were in shambles.

Treasured Internal Processes

Within each of our personal mythologies, there is a treasured internal process that we believe keeps us and our myth safe. Every myth also has a core fear and a core desire. Let's go back to Jeff:

Personal mythology:	I am special.
Treasured internal process:	Anything outside me is suspect.
Core fear:	I'm not good enough; I am nothing.
Core desire:	To be loved and recognized for who I am.

Often the easiest thing to identify is the core fear or core desire. Listen to what you say and the attitude you express and then reverse it. Jeff's favorite lines are: "I'm just a regular guy" and "I don't care if you agree with me." His attitude is one of friendly superiority. Therein lies the self-deception.

Here is another example:

Personal mythology: I am in charge.

Treasured internal process: I am not satisfied with the efforts of others, which always fall short.

Core fear: I am powerless.

Core desire: To feel worthy.

And another:

Personal mythology: I am responsible and independent.

Treasured internal process: I have no needs; I take care of others.

Core fear: Annihilation.

Core desire: To be dependent.

You can often best find your personal mythology in how others see you and, most especially, how you were seen as a child: the helper, the boss, the wonder child, the fragile one, the sensitive one, the artistic one.

Crisis often challenges our personal mythology, if not threatens it to the core. Jeff found out that he was not so special that he was exempt from society's or life's rules.

Luckily for him, few mistakes are irrevocable. He was finally able to accept the help of his friends. They showed
him the rules and helped him follow them. In the process
of healing his life, he also addressed his core fear or desire.
Without being "special," in his messiest self, he was loved,
cared for, and embraced.

Answer the following questions:

- What was your strongest single belief about your-
  self before your crisis?
- What is your tagline, the line you use when your be-
  liefs or ideas are challenged?
- What is your best personal quality?
- What is your worst personal quality?

Now play with your answers. Reverse them. Pretend they
are true about everyone in your life except you. Pretend
you are sitting with yourself and you are both competing
for who is the most —— or the least ——.

Ask your friends to fill in your mythology question-
naire for you.

- What is my personal mythology?
- What way of dealing with the world is most constant for me?
- What is my worst fear?
- What is my greatest desire?

If they hit the target, you will know. If they miss the target, you will know. Learn to understand your personal mythology. It will not take a day, and it may be an ongoing process. This mythology is the style of being that you are leaving to begin anew. Once upon a time your personal myth saved your life. Jeff would have been destroyed by the violence and neglect in his home had he not insisted that he were special and looked for unique experiences and forms of expression to sustain the myth. But like all living things, we grow, and the myths that once fueled you can now imprison you.

Contemplate what your personal mythology is taking from you now. Jeff's personal mythology was not allowing him to use what he had built in his life to create stability, family, success, and joy. As he ignored the responsibility of his creation, what should have been his support — his fine work — dissolved beneath him, offering a springboard to grow from, much like his childhood home.

- If your personal mythology is one of independence, you are not getting the nourishment you need to grow.
- If your personal mythology is one of being in charge, you are not getting the acknowledgment you need to find your real strength.
- If you are in crisis, your old myth is no longer working for you and it is time to read the story, write "the end," and start a new and more pleasurable story in your life.

❧

Your personal mythology may be overly sunny (you denial types) or overly self-pitying (anger types) and unrepresentative of your life — such as someone with a lovely personal mythology who is lacking essential elements in his or her life — love, money, job satisfaction, health, and so on. If your personal mythology has you cast as either Mother Teresa or Satan, you probably need to talk it out with someone to get some perspective. You need to look and see whether your personal mythology matches your life.

Revising Your Personal Mythology

When you consciously and courageously choose to grieve and move on, you rewrite your story not only for yourself but also for those around you.

A player who might have filled the role of critical father may now, because you have rewritten your shared drama, play the role of inspiring ally. Your rejecting ex-spouse may play the role of helper with your child or may hold the memories for you that you no longer want to keep but want to touch every now and then. Your boss may go from unreasonable, unsupportive employer to powerful teacher and ally. All because you've redefined your personal story, your personal mythology.

Now is the time to rewrite your personal mythology consciously. We tend to create from what we were. I challenge you to create from what you *choose* to be. A time of crisis is ideal for rewriting your personal mythology. You are in the moment between one story's end and another's beginning. You can choose to continue your old theme (as you have done so many times before), or you can rewrite the story, starting right now, and in doing so heal every aspect of your future.

᠔

Jeff's new personal mythology:	I have something to offer the world. My voice must be heard.
Treasured internal process:	Taking care of the details that support my creation. Safety.
Core fear:	Failure.
Core desire:	To be acknowledged.

This myth, too, will one day become obsolete for Jeff but not until he has accomplished its goal.

Jeff's saga has a postscript. The dentist found an abscess in his tooth that he believed had been there for over a decade. It was treated, and Jeff's exhaustion and hair-trigger temper diminished considerably. Jeff's business is doing great, and he is starting a family with a woman he loves. Every once in a while, Jeff resents having to deal with regular meals, taxes, exercise, and dental and medical visits, just like the rest of us. Then he reminds himself to look around his life and value the foundation for home, family, and success that these efforts have brought him.

꙳

If you are an anger type who feels that your best efforts are met with ingratitude or rejection, reserve your best efforts for yourself only or for when you simply choose to, but do manage your anger. If you are a depression type whose personal mythology finds life overwhelming, find one small thing that you can master and take hope in (walking up one flight of stairs, going out to coffee at a coffee shop each morning, putting on lipstick).

An anger type's personal mythology may go like this: I work my butt off day after day and then I come home, and nothing is the way I need it to be. My kids are ungrateful, my wife unresponsive, and my boss a slave master.

A new mythology might be: I find my own contentment. What I do in life I do for myself although there are always trade-offs, but I always come out ahead. My passion, when it gets to be too much, is directed toward physical activity and work, which makes me healthy, handsome, and successful. My energy is envied by all. I appreciate myself, and because of that, I end up surrounded by people who appreciate me.

Exercise: How to Rewrite Your Personal Mythology

Take a moment right now to become aware of your own story, the one that you are relinquishing — or possibly the one that has been taken from you. To get to your core essence, reduce your story to a single sentence. Long-suffering woman gives all for love. Poor boy makes good. Brilliant woman misunderstood and unappreciated by the world.

This one-sentence story will be a huge oversimplification, of course, but it will tell you a lot about which experiences you select to define yourself.

Now write a new one-sentence story: this time consciously compose a story about the life you want to live, about the self you want to be. Passionate lover lives her dreams. Lucky man has the Midas touch on Wall Street. Brilliant man shares insights with a welcoming world.

You can ask your good friends to give snapshot descriptions of you. Sometimes it takes a friend's perspective to see yourself clearly.

Once you've completed your updated story, try acting it out — actually living this story. Living out your new story may not be easy. You may be having trouble finding the energy to get off your couch or even to put one foot in front of the other. If so just *pretend* that you are embodying your new story. You will notice immediate and dramatic changes in your life.

Remember the anecdote I shared about the scientist Niels Bohr and the good-luck horseshoe hanging over his front door? You don't have to *believe* your new story for it to work; you just have to pretend.

Rewriting your story will not change your sense of self and sense of identity overnight, but it will begin the process. Psychologists know that we act in ways consistent with our self-image. Simply by rewriting your story, you will start — in little ways at first — to act consistently with what you have written.

Your Get-Out-of-Jail-Free Card

You are not a prisoner of your habits. Usually the external enemy, a person or a situation, is not really the enemy. The enemy is anyone or anything that keeps you from moving through a crisis to a new beginning or slows your travel time.

We all tend to have the same problems, trip on the same cracks in every situation. We re-create a story line over and over — until we have resolved it. That is how the subconscious works. You will get into the same situation again if you don't recognize the dynamic that you attract and work to change it. Crisis allows you the opportunity to create new relationships that sustain you and to introduce changes into existing relationships.

Of course, no two relationships or situations are identical, but they often share similar qualities, beginning and ending in a certain way. For example, all your relationships may involve your caretaking the other person and not getting your needs met. Or perhaps your relationships may all start off intensely and end in one or both of you losing interest in the other. If you had to make a statement about what happens in all of your relationships, what would that be?

Here's how to stop this cycle for the last time and keep the jailers out of your life.

1) Recognize your pattern in past relationships.
2) Gracefully change that pattern in current relationships.
3) Be aware of your pattern in all new relationships.
4) Take responsibility for the fact that you are not a victim of your pattern. You have gotten your needs (albeit probably not healthy or conscious ones) met through the relationships you have attracted. Recognize those needs and fill them in other ways.

You have played the old tape for too long. It's time you found another tape.

Exercise: Consulting Your Inner Guide

This powerful exercise will help you rewrite your new mythology as you sleep and carry its power and effectiveness into your life.

One of the things I have learned from my many years of working as a practicing intuitive is that each of us has the wisdom to find our way. Sometimes we are closer to this inner guide than at other times; sometimes we can consciously hear its voice. In times of change we urgently need the clarity and certainty our intuition brings.

Our thinking may be shocked, disorganized, hopeless, paranoid, and a host of other things, but intuition allows us to move through the disorder and into clarity. When you think of little children who survive in war, find food, shelter, community, you see the power of intuitive guidance.

The following exercise should be done nightly and will help you be guided by the part of you that is solid, sane, and whole. This exercise should be done before bed and will take only a moment. If you have a particularly challenging day, you can also do this exercise and take a brief nap to reset your intuitive focus and your inner program to keep you on the right track.

Sleep is a wonderful time for both intuition and the subconscious to work. Your awareness and your five senses, which are involved during the day in evaluating your environment, are free during sleep to deal with the complexities of your life. In sleep you can experience and integrate the changes that you made during your waking hours. You can also search the intelligence of your world for the information and support that you need to create your goal.

To do this exercise, you first need to find an object that you carry with you always. It can be a piece of jewelry, your wallet, your cell phone, your keys, anything that you always have with you.

Before you go to sleep, hold this object and state your goal. Then put the object somewhere you can reach it or on your body so during the night, if you wish, you can feel its presence.

Again, don't worry if you can't see how your goal is possible, or even if your only goal at the moment is to feel better or simply to be out of your current situation. Clarity will come with time.

If you can, use your senses to experience your goal as already true. Feel, taste, smell, see (inside you and around you), hear, know that your goal has already come true. Don't get stuck on the details.

Each time you do this exercise, your experience of it

will change, depending on your mood, your day, the insights your intuition had the previous night, and the maturity gained by your subconscious in this process. Don't be shaken by the challenges that come up in your thoughts and feelings to your goal. Unless you are in total denial, you will experience some awareness, each time you do this exercise, of all the reasons that intuition cannot happen. You will experience all of your stored doubts from the archives of your memory and subconscious.

Believe it or not, these doubts are a good thing. You will work through these issues as you sleep and will awaken with greater clarity. As you move through crisis to your goal, you will find that there is less and less interference when you do this exercise. When there is none, you have arrived at your goal.

During the night, your intuition will search for your best moves in the world as your subconscious works on your patterning to allow you to make these moves, act, and respond successfully. The object will act as an on switch for your intuition during your active, waking hours. You will be conditioned, in a sense hypnotized, to go into a productive, intuitive, aware state when you touch the object. If you have to make decisions or respond quickly, you will find yourself automatically touching this object; when you do so you will have a sense of clarity and direction.

The results of this exercise are not magic. We are creatures of keys and patterns, and the essential element in resilience is to create strong keys to ignite powerful and positive patterns. This object is not an irreplaceable lucky charm. If you lose it you can create another key by patterning yourself with a different object. You create your own luck, and you can ground yourself firmly on the path of good fortune. This exercise will make choosing in your best interest a part of your subconscious, everyday pattern, and day by day you will find your new life.

DECIDING WHO YOU WANT TO BE

Making a Final Break

During your transition to the life you are creating, you have been digesting the losses of your crisis only a bit at a time. Research shows that continually processing your crisis actually harms you by forcing your brain to undergo the initial trauma again and again. Schedule times for introspection and activities to follow it for assimilation.

Crisis is contagious. So is health. Know the reaction

WELCOME TO YOUR CRISIS

types of the people you live and work with. Notice the reaction types in your birth family and the ways in which
your type may have been influenced by theirs and perhaps
still is. Families are great teachers. You experience families
over an extended period in various stages of evolution and
revolution.

When you are aware of type, you can respond to those
close to you in affirming and healing ways. You can maintain healthy, dynamic, passionate relationships through the
many challenges that life always offers. You can teach your
children to be resilient and to honor their unique responses and gifts, while giving them the tools to thrive and
to help others do the same. We are all healers in the process of healing. Awareness and connectedness are the elements that activate the alchemy of change.

Reality Check

If you look at a spot on the wall for too long, it begins to
distort. Look at one thing and notice the distortion.

Where in your current situation has your focus been

stuck? What do you think has been distorted in your thinking and behavior because of this? What could you focus on that would be more empowering to you in building your new life?

৵

At this point in your journey, the healthy cores of the response types come together to help you create the final break from the crisis you have left behind. They now serve you to protect the new life you have created and to help you and your life be adaptive to future changes. Now you can use the energy of rage, anxiety, depression, and denial in their healthy, life-affirming incarnations, without being overwhelmed.

These elements of protection, once learned, will mitigate the damage from any similar assaults in the future. Each response type has a state of injury, a state of grace, and a state of function. The state of injury is an automatic, habitual response to any threat or loss. The state of grace is the unique gift that consciously dealing with the healing of the injury brings you. The state of function is the part of each type that we all need to survive and thrive and which creates, protects, and rebuilds our self.

Part of the task of crisis is to address not only the current challenges, but also the more insidious challenges that got you into the situation in the first place. The challenge of crisis is evolution, reaching a new, more effective, and more joyous state of being. You can use the positive core of the four types to protect your well-being, predict and direct change, and live consciously in the present.

- Using the positive core of denial, you now push aside any truly indigestible aspects of your crisis: what cannot be processed and what perhaps does not serve you to process. Some assaults on our self should not and cannot be understood, and these losses need to be left behind and dissolved using the positive core of denial.
- Using the positive core of depression, you now give up the fight against loss and allow yourself to sink into your new self, your new life, and your new world. You are able to release the way your energy

has been directed at the past and settle fully into the present.

+ Using the positive core of anxiety, you hesitate appropriately when encountering situations that may cause you harm or pull you back into the crisis that you are leaving behind. You are able to use your sense of fear intuitively to keep from falling back into old behaviors and relationships or from engaging in situations that can cause you pain.

+ Using the positive core of rage, you refuse to be injured as you have been in the past. You create appropriate boundaries where you may have been hesitant to create them before. When you betray yourself by not protecting yourself appropriately, you experience rage.

Mark Twain once advised us that when we are angry, we should count to ten slowly — and *then* swear. Twain was being facetious, of course, but all great humor is based on profound truth. Our emotions all serve positive functions in our human being, but we must be their master and not allow them to master us. You are capable of making choices that nourish and protect your life.

You do not have to believe in yourself. Sometimes that is an impossible task. You simply have to put one foot in front of the other and give yourself the time, space, skills, and forgiveness to find your right direction once again.

Creating Your Future

You have, up until this point, been removing the obstacles to your evolving self. You have been dealing with a new set of realities, challenges, perceptions, and ways of being. There has been little time, energy, space to set new goals or dream of a new life.

The good news is that no matter how lost you may feel, you are already halfway home. The energy that you have directed toward restructuring yourself and orienting yourself in your new world has already taken you so much closer to the birth of your new self.

My favorite quote from *Grist for the Mill*, by Ram Dass,

is, "The pain of birth is the pain of death and the pain of death is the pain of birth." At the same time you have been letting go of your old life, you have been building your new one.

When you are focused on your crisis, all of your energy is going toward what you want to move away from. Reread the last sentence. You — and you are your energy and focus — are moving toward what you want to move *away* from. You need now to move toward what you want to create, even if you don't yet know what that is, and deal with what you want to move away from in the process.

Crisis usually comes upon us uninvited. The conscious mind is taken by surprise. The subconscious needs to know why it should bother constructing something new when everything is so vulnerable to change and loss. The obvious answer is that life must go on. For a soul in pain, however, that truism often fails to motivate us fully. We, however, need to engage with all of our resources and intention in the powerful act of creation.

Healing the Future

We can heal the future because we are creating the future now, in this moment. It is perhaps easier to heal the future, where infinite possibilities still exist, than to heal the past. We tend to focus on our losses and mistakes and spend inordinate and unhealthy amounts of energy on "what if" or "if only," when what was no longer exists. It is fuel only for what will be.

That does not mean that you cannot heal the wounds of the past. By using techniques such as intuitive dialog, you are doing just that. Your focus, however, is on the moment — on what remains and what you are creating, by choice, now.

Often we are stuck in the past because we imagine our power, our love, our beauty, our fortune resides there. We cling to these memories as though, by sheer desire and remorse, we could resurrect them. We feel powerless to create what we have lost again in our lives. You are right. You cannot re-create the past, if for no other reason than that you yourself have changed.

You can, however, create in the future everything you

valued in yourself and the world that has been lost to you. It will be different. Unbelievably, it will be more powerful, moving, and satisfying than anything you can imagine now because you have made the choice to grow (or perhaps the world has made the choice for you). I can make that statement with absolute certainty. You would not have this book in your hand right now if this were not true — even if you reason that the book was lying on a table and you just happened to pick it up, through no conscious choice of your own. I would say to you that we are always making a choice, conscious or not of what we are choosing. You have chosen to create and heal your future in the here and now.

Our most satisfying dreams are the ones we *create* — not the ones we cling to.

❧

What if you could leave every mistake, injustice, illness, and sadness in a suitcase on the sidewalk and walk away from it? You wouldn't even have to "start again," you could simply be fresh and new and ready to create whatever you wanted and take advantage of every opportunity that life has to offer. It might feel strange, lonely, vulnerable, and perhaps even disloyal. You would, however, be free to create and experience anything at all, even a better version of what you just had to leave behind.

Do you know how much time you invest in carrying that suitcase around every day, remembering its contents or worse, having a stray part of your luggage get in the way right at the very moment when you could have a good time or say yes to a situation that wouldn't normally match your luggage?

Right now, in this moment, you are creating what comes next. You can even change this moment as you live it. You can make yourself more comfortable, get a pillow, order food, find a good, hopeful thought and experience it. You can call someone who makes you feel good or do something that you have been putting off for days, weeks, or months.

You are not stuck being who you have been until this moment. You are not doomed to the elements in life that displease you. Your history, your situation at present is something you have the consciousness and the ability not only to change but also to walk away from. You have some choices to make, right now, in this moment. You can continue in the pattern that you have been following.

I can hear your questions. What if I have a chronic illness? What if I have lost all of my money? What if my husband just asked for a divorce? What if I had a traumatic childhood and am so damaged that I cannot create anything sound in my life?

These are all things that you have endured until this moment. You are defining yourself by these situations. These situations have happened to you, perhaps are happening now, but they are not you. As long as you insist this is true, you can change it all right now. If you are ill, choose not to live life as an ill person but as a healthy person with an illness that you are walking away from. Do not hold on to the money, job, or love that you have already lost. Use those same hands to embrace the present and reach toward the future.

Your options are limited or infinite, depending on your perspective. In the many years that I have taught my last book, *The Circle*, to thousands of people, I have seen lives that seemed destroyed, found too late, shattered, or worse, lives that never really happened. Many of these lives were created anew with a simple change in perspective and the powerful redirection of energy and resources that this change creates.

Exercise: Attracting Your Future

Whether you feel it or not, you are on your way to mastering the current situation and creating a new life. This does not mean that it is clear sailing from here on in. It means that if you maintain, even imperfectly, the steps you have taken thus far, you will find that your world is changing for the better and in ways that will surprise you and renew your faith in your life and in yourself. You will look back on this time as the turning point in your life, the point at which you were mastering yourself and creating your future.

Sometimes we almost seem to step into the *perfect* situation. We meet the ideal mate. Or we find the job that "makes" our career. Or we invest in the right stock.

In fact these "moments" of serendipity were planned and prepared for by your subconscious long before you "fell" into them. There are many perfect situations that you are passing by right now (don't worry, there are always more opportunities) because you are not yet prepared to attract, recognize, or accept them. You are not yet the person who can connect with your particular "perfect situation." Fortunately, we are about to change that right now by healing your future.

As you read the next passage, follow my directions with your imagination at the same time. You may see what you imagine or feel, hear, or sense it in some other way. Don't judge how well you imagine; simply follow along. You may not sense anything at all. Don't worry; your subconscious is doing the work even if you cannot now perceive it.

The first few times that you do this exercise, don't take notes or try to remember what you are experiencing. As you become accustomed to this exercise, you will be able to do it without interference from your conscious mind, and you will want to take notes, as they will contain valuable information about your future. Don't worry; the information is stored, anyway, in that favorite cluttered closet: your subconscious mind.

Find a time when you won't be interrupted. Expect

some distractions, such as noise from the outside, the phone ringing, even your own thoughts. Prepare yourself mentally to let these distractions move through you without effect.

Find a comfortable position, take a long deep breath, and exhale slowly. Repeat this breath a few times. As you do, give yourself the suggestion that what you accomplish here, in this moment, will affect not only you but also the world around you. You will be finding your way, making a map of your journey tomorrow. You will not be able to change the facts of the moment. Your life right now is simply the way it is, and you will be starting from a place of accepting those realities. You will, however, be able to encounter new people, situations, and bits of good fortune that will take you to your true, real, and ideal home.

When you are ready imagine yourself walking along a path. You start here and now, but as you walk, your feet take you to the exact place where you need to be. You don't need to know where you are going. You will get there no matter what because it is, it has always been, your true destination.

As you walk notice the people you meet and the events that you witness. You don't have to remember them, just notice what is going on around you and how it changes you on your journey. As you journey you may find things or gain powers that enable you to journey more easily and comfortably. You may take anything that you find along with you.

You may notice that with each exhalation you are releasing expectations and confusions from your past. You may feel a sense of lightness in your mind, body, and spirit. You are becoming empty, and yet you are also filled with your own divine connection, your true connection to all that exists around you.

As you feel the power of this energy, you sense your destination approaching. Now you have arrived.

You don't have to know where you are. It is enough to know that you have arrived and that this is exactly where you needed to be. You are home in the most powerful and exquisite sense of the word, and here you are truly your most powerful and joyful self. All that you need is around you, and you have all of the qualities that this situation requires.

You now understand the past and what it taught you to enable you to arrive at this exquisite, perfect moment. The past is a precious gem that you hold in your hands. It is no longer one with you, and yet it is something that you still possess, to use in this moment now.

Allow yourself to become fully present in this moment of completion, of arrival, and know that you have just charted your path to your perfect destination. Even if, in this moment, you cannot feel, see, or understand where you are, the part of you that guides and determines your life now knows which way to go. You will find that the instinctual part of you — the part that moves correctly even when you don't have conscious understanding — will prepare you to encounter the perfect moments that you are drawing to you, perfectly. Your experience of your own preparedness, your own wisdom will give you the ability to walk with surety and grace every moment of every day.

Every time you do this exercise, you will be patterning a new and powerful future for yourself. In addition, your intuition and subconscious will be "looking ahead" to whatever difficult situations you might encounter and preparing you to find the tools to deal with them effectively or avoid them altogether in advance.

You may, after a while, get valuable and accurate information about your future from this exercise. After the exercise write down the details that you remember. The greatest proof of intuition occurs when you, yourself, retrieve accurate future data and you have documented proof that this data came to you before the event. Documenting is important because when you know that you have the ability to predict and to use this foresight to change outcomes, you will use it more powerfully in your life.

The goal of this exercise, however, is not to remember the information, but rather to allow intuition to repattern the subconscious for success. If you remember nothing, respect this as your unique process and know that the exercise is doing its job anyway.

The first few times you do this exercise, you may find that your focus is more on bringing back something you lost than allowing for something new to come in. This will change as you repeat the exercise and intuition guides you to the greatest possibilities that exist for you and to recognize what no longer exists in your life. You may find yourself bringing events from your past back in different ways, ways that are possible and practical for your future.

After you have done this exercise a few times, it will take you less than a minute to complete. It is helpful to perform this exercise a few times during the day, as it will also help you prepare for and redirect the daily experiences that you encounter. You will have a different experience every time you do this exercise. If you don't you are cutting off your inner ability to create and direct energy in favor of a reassuring pattern. If this happens simply change a single element of how and where you do this exercise. Do it in the shower, on the train, add music (change the music after a few sessions), sit in a different location, do something, anything, differently to break the pattern. When you break a pattern, you gift yourself with innovation.

೩

Good lives are not easy. They require daily acts of adaptation, courage, and love. One of my agent's favorite sayings is, "It isn't easy being easy!"

೩

You can put your focus on working through your past. You can also decide to simply be different, attract different experiences, and make different choices beginning now. You will work through your past by refusing to allow it to control your present. That commitment in itself will bring the pertinent pieces of your past to consciousness for inspection and resolution.

Right now, in this moment, decide what you are creating. It does not have to be the whole pie. It may, in this moment, be a simple detail such as to be able to take a breath without feeling pain or to have enough money to pay your rent. Know that once you decide it, you begin to create it, because your resources are now directed toward that goal.

It is not necessary for you to believe what I am going to say in the next section. The practices in this book that are based on this concept will work for you whether you believe in them or not. I am always suspicious of things that require belief. If something works it should work regardless of your "faith" in its effectiveness. As long as you use the practices, with or without belief, these truths will change your life. Then, perhaps, if it is useful to you, you will believe.

 Energy connects us to everything around us. You are sending out new signals and attracting new information and experiences. When you perform subtle shifts in perception as I have described above, your life changes in dramatic ways. Try it now. Decide that you are creating a new reality now. The past is behind you, and when it comes up, its purpose is to give you a greater understanding of how to proceed in the future.

Unlike the experience of the three R's, your patterns and memories are available to you now only to inform you better of your choices in forward movement. You are healing the future by living differently in this moment. Simple. Powerful. This truth will prove itself to you.

You can leave something or someone and have it come back to you in a new way. In fact that is the only route of return. Something in the past is, by definition, gone. The future is, by definition, something that you are creating now.

Who Do You Want to Be?

Today, right now, in this moment, as you read this sentence, you are creating your next moment. The way you breathe, your thoughts, where your intuition is traveling, how you are sitting, everything you do and everything you are is predicting what you will *become.*

The powerful life is lived experiencing today and creating tomorrow with direction and intention.

❧

Who are you? We've returned to this question throughout the book.

If you had to describe yourself to someone who needed "the real you," what would you say?

Take a moment to write a few descriptive sentences or paragraphs about yourself. If you are in crisis or going through major change, write about who you were *before* the upheaval.

Here are some examples:

- I am the mother of two children. I spend most of my time doing things to help them grow up to be successful and happy people. I enjoy painting, and I hope that it will one day be a career. I am not as organized as I would like to be and often leave impor-

WELCOME TO YOUR CRISIS

tant tasks undone. I am a warm host, and people love to be at my house.

- I have a small but successful real-estate firm that I have built from the ground up. I excel at matching people and habitats. I love my home, and I entertain frequently. I have begun to dabble in interior design. I grew up in the Midwest, and I have enjoyed my big-city life.
- I am a beautiful young woman. My physical beauty has been both a source of power and pleasure and a source of pain. I turn thirty this year. I am in great shape, and I have so many dreams that I have trouble picking just one. I want to have a family, but I fall in and out of love every few months, and I just can't decide with whom I want to have a family.

I am sure that looking at these descriptions you can think of hundreds of things that could change these outward manifestations of self.

Consulting Your Inner Community

You are choosing right now who you are going to be. You need to begin a conscious dialog with your inner community.

You are not one solid, cohesive, monolithic whole. As a human being you comprise an inner community. Many ways of being, perceiving, deciding, and reacting come together in a staggering act of unity to create every single response and reaction that you have.

As you saw from the test at the beginning of the book, your inner community includes the following:

- the you who reacts
- the you who bases her feelings and responses on experience that may or may not actually represent the current situation
- the intellectual you who knows information, statistics, other people's stories, and all other kinds of knowledge, which may or may not be correct, about your current experience

- the transcendent you who can take a bird's-eye, dis-
  passionate view of the situation and evaluate it
  without judgment or emotion in the context of the
  larger picture of life
- the idealistic you who wishes things were different
  so hard it hurts and the pessimistic you who ex-
  pected the worst and is shocked to still be standing
- the intuitive you who has a sense of what is coming
  up in the future and who understands everyone
  else's perspective

There are many more of you not listed here. With so many
of you to deal with in your inner community, how do you
create unity of thought, feeling, and action to accomplish
change? Make a short list of who is in your inner community. The doubter, the princess, the healer, the frightened
child, the bulldozer. Take a short journey from babyhood to
present and note some of the people you meet within you.

- Who has the strongest voice?
- Who are you afraid to listen to?

- Who has gotten you in trouble in the past?
- Who comforts you?

Everyone in your inner community has a say in everything you do. The pecking order, however, changes with goals, will, health, and awareness. You want your inner community to organize around your positive goals and not around your fears or destructive impulses.

In order to accomplish this, you need to master the most impulsive, unconscious of the group first, as you did in the beginning of this book by working with your reaction type. Without mastering the impulsive you, it is difficult to create the positive experiences that will teach you to rely automatically on the others in your inner community. Your first and primary task is always to take care of your reaction type. You are then free to manage your inner community in a mindful, conscious, and positive manner.

- What is your positive dream?
- Who in your community can help you create your dream?
- Who gets in the way?

Now you can't just ignore those selves within you who get in the way. It's not as if you can just "kick them out." You need to listen to what they need from the rest of you to be able to trust the community to take care of them. This dialog will require real effort from you. As a writer I love to put things on paper. Try writing down the conversations you have with your various selves, the added advantage being that you can look back at it and see just how brilliant and in touch you really were, even in your darkest hour.

However, you can also do this aloud, to yourself, with a friend, drawing pictures of the people and interactions. Use anything that works for you. The important thing is not just to communicate with your many selves but also, going forward, to be able to maintain an awareness of these selves.

Talk to yourself, perhaps not on the street, perhaps not in public, but talk to yourself and listen. You have the answers. There is no "figuring out" involved. Your inner community will tell you what you need, how to proceed, what tools you have that you may have forgotten or never been introduced to, and an infinite amount of other things, if you just make the time and space to listen.

Remember, awareness is everything. Everyone has the strength to use awareness to create change. Even without effort, simple awareness of who within us can guide us to safety will create an automatic choice to hear that voice and bide its counsel.

Things are bridges between the unseen world and the world we are creating in our life, on earth, in "reality." When you take an idea or concept from your imagination and implement it in the world, creating it in some tangible form, it is an extremely powerful map for the subconscious, your intuition, your intellect, and perhaps for the mobilization of the energy of the universe around you.

Take time every day to do what I call in *The Circle* a "reality tale." Make up a short story of what your ideal life is and move the elements around until they fit. Slowly, surely, you will create this new life.

Reconnecting with
Your Original Self

It is hard not to look at an infant and think wistfully of a time long ago, when we shared its purity and innocence as infants ourselves. So much of growing up seems to involve losing touch with our pristine self.

The real you — your innocent, courageous self at birth, the being you were always meant to be — is not lost. You refused to cut off this special part of you in a way that would damage it and hid it safely inside. We hide this precious part from the world to protect it from turmoil and damage. We take what we truly value and keep it safe — not realizing that, in doing so, we hide it even from ourselves.

Only the rarest children lead blessed lives and do not encounter situations in which they need to hide their treasure. Beneath all the layers of defense, it still lies, untouched. You made sure that, no matter what, your pristine, original self would be safe and intact.

Remarkably, crisis forces us to get back in touch with this lost part of ourselves. We need *all* of our resources to get us through a major life upheaval, and so crisis becomes a positive, transformative force in our lives.

Though those defenses kept your essence intact through many different life experiences, you are strong enough now to break those defenses down. You are so close, having arrived at this point — here, in this moment — to finding a way back to your original self and to bringing it forth in all its miraculous glory to create your new life.

I want to tell you a story. You will find its truth in your experience of this book, as well as in the crises you have successfully navigated and transformed in the past.

Once upon a time there was a child: you. This child may have had perfect parents or dreadful ones. You may have been born to a safe and secure life or to a violent, dysfunctional one, or somewhere in the middle. Whoever you were, wherever you were, there was a point early in your life when you took the things that were most precious to you about yourself and gave them extra shelter and protection. You may even have hidden what was truly of value to you and about you.

As you got older and your armoring of self became more structured, these precious gems of self moved deeper within you — so deep that even you forget they are there or were ever a part of you. As an adult, you often build your life without the use or awareness of these personal treasures and hungers.

Then crisis hits. In order to survive and evolve, you need more of yourself than you have allowed yourself to be in the past. You need to dig deeply within, and when you do you find, no matter how insignificant or worthless you may feel in that moment, a treasure chest containing all that you truly value and all that you truly are.

If, in that moment, you provide yourself with some

basic support such as is outlined in this book, you will be able to unearth some buried treasures from deep within yourself, bringing these treasures to your conscious, active, adult life, enriching it and you in ways you had forgotten to imagine. Talents, values, and things that you had lived your life to date without will be salvaged in that expedition. In fact, without crisis you would not need to reach into that chest to survive intact, and the likelihood of your finding your soul's desire and filling it would diminish.

To give your heart and soul completely over to an endeavor that requires you to endure pain, loss, or even change, you need something worthwhile at the end of the challenge. At the end of this challenge, you will have created a life more wonderful than anything that you can imagine now, lived by a human being more precious, useful, and talented than you have ever known. You will have opened the treasure chest in which you hid your most sacred self. You will have found home.

If you look back on your past crises, you will often find that you acquired a piece of yourself — your happiness, and your ability to get what you truly wanted from the world — directly from that crisis. If you cannot find those memories, this book has been and is about creating them now.

Yes, a crisis can be great enough to destroy, but only if you are unwilling to let go of what is already lost and move forward, one step at a time, toward a new reality. The more committed and able you are to achieve this forward movement, the more of what you truly want and need will be created in your life.

Your Inviolate Self

Some inner qualities, however, can never be changed. They can be injured, buried, hidden, or distorted in some other way, but they always remain. Some of these qualities include the need and capacity for the following:

- love
- stimulation
- forgiveness

- pleasure
- connection and understanding
- nurturing
- creativity and creation
- motivation
- insight
- healing and soothing

These are some of your inalienable capacities and needs as a human being. You are gifted with and are valued for one or more of the things on this list. These are the constants that remain during a crisis, and from which you will build a new and more authentic life and definition of self.

Review this list and notice where you are functioning in these areas. These are the seeds of your future. The description you patch together from the preceding list will serve as possible indicators of the new you.

This description of how and why you function is now up for grabs. You do not know the new description yet, and the one that you have, if you are in crisis, is a description of the state of crisis and not of you. You can now decide who you will become. In each moment you choose your future. Anything can change, right now, if you have the tools of transformation.

Before your crisis, for example, you may have nurtured others by giving selflessly while denying your own needs. Crisis may be revolutionizing the way that you nurture. You may find that you nurture now more with your insight than with your elbow grease.

You may find that during crisis, you are finding no outlet for connection and understanding. This is you-in-crisis, not the real you. If this was descriptive of you before your crisis, perhaps crisis is driving you to find inroads to interpersonal relationships and other support in your life.

Needs are powerful motivators. You will find them. The you-in-crisis is the you in a state of transformation. Now is the time to choose to be the person you want to be, not the person who emerged simply owing to the influences of nature and nurture.

&

I was the eldest of four children. I was a solid, responsible child with a lovely but mentally ill mother and an overwhelmed physician father. I grew up being a navy blue child. I did not wear pink; I would have felt like an imposter. If you hurt me, I did not cry. I did not work hard, and I did not aim for much except the structures of safety and solidity that I could find. I wasn't particularly talented at anything other than taking care of other people, most especially my mother. I didn't sleep over at other children's houses, and my only real intimate contact was my mother. She was the magic in my life. She was beauty and truth and reason. My one and only love.

Then, as I said earlier, when I was fourteen my mother committed suicide. This was after a divorce in which I'd sided with my mother against my father. I was left in the custody of my father, who for the past many years, had been my archenemy.

In order to survive my loss, I had to escape. Being responsible no longer had much value now that the object of my responsibility — my mother — was gone. I retreated into myself. I wrote poetry. I read books to be transported to another place to help me tolerate the pain of my loss. I began reaching toward my mother with my imagination. I reached within me to a state where my world and my mother's world would meet.

It is now thirty-three years after my great loss. I am still responsible and able to take care of others. I have added to these values the treasure of my imagination and my ability to transcend the borders between worlds, such as the world of science and the world of intuition.

A crisis forced me to find new resources to survive and thrive. Although many other crises have given me other gifts, this first gift of crisis is what defines me professionally to this day.

People walk into my house, see me working in my pajamas in my little blue room filled with scents and color, drinking milky coffee with my animals around me and my son popping in and out, and say, "I wish I had your life." I wonder how many people would have said that to the withdrawn, abandoned, fourteen-year-old wearing navy blue without an ounce of charm in her solid little body.

I no longer miss my mother because to have her would mean to give up the treasures her loss gave me. And half my wardrobe is pink.

The Gift of Limitations

Crisis offers us the *gift* of limitations. In crisis, we must use all of our resources effectively. We have no room to waste time, energy, money, thought, or even feeling on anything inessential.

You have to strip down to what is truly essential to deal effectively with the moment at hand. The gift of this, as you will find, is that you create, become, and surround yourself with what you truly love and value.

Believe me, during crisis you are often experiencing the most difficult part of yourself. You feel that everything important is being lost. The loss itself feels annihilating. You are probably not sitting around, reading this book thinking, "Wow, I am constructing a truly meaningful and authentic life." The process does not have to feel good to work.

You choose how you end up in life. In decades of working with people, I have found one great truth: when you know what you value, you achieve it. If there is any such thing as destiny, this is it. The stripping away of everything that we thought we needed is not usually a pleasant process. The rewards, however, are wondrous.

Every crisis allows true authenticity. In fact often we don't have many of our old resources available to us, and we are forced back to a place we had forgotten, a place of fundamental values and truths. We carry with us many counterfeit needs and beliefs. We acquire them over time from our parents, our society, our friends, our loves.

A unique being with unique gifts and needs resides in each one of us. I have seen thousands of people in my career from the inside out, and every person amazes me in his or her miraculous originality. When we live through our authenticity, the part of us that is uniquely ours, we create exactly the life we want.

Getting to that point, however, often takes the painful ripping away of false self. Just because something is inauthentic or even unhealthy does not mean that you are not profoundly attached to it. Although we can achieve an authentic life relatively painlessly over decades of evolution, crisis speeds the process to an instant.

Revolution, however, has its own rewards. The miraculous power of the healing we create through crisis can be as stunning as looking at the sun.

The Gift of Need

You will be receiving many gifts of self as a result of having to dig deeply into yourself to resolve a crisis or change. Perhaps the greatest gift of all is the gift of need. In crisis we need a new set of gifts from the world and the people around us. Often the cause of the crisis is our subconscious need to receive things that we did not receive in childhood, things that we don't even know exist, in order to become truly fulfilled human beings. Crisis forces us to reach for the things we did not get in childhood because we need these resources to survive.

No matter how perfect or imperfect your childhood was, there are always essential yet unfilled needs; this is the nature of childhood. Your unfulfilled need may be for unconditional love. Or your unmet need may be for intellectual stimulation, a strong sense of self, autonomy, the ability to rely on the strengths of others, a sense of pleasure and safety in your own body, or even the right to exist. After a while, we learned to cut off our hunger for these things.

To resolve a crisis successfully, you are always called

upon to fill needs unmet for your entire life. Suddenly you are in a situation in which, for the first time in your life, you must rely on the support of others and allow other people to take care of you. Perhaps you need to ask for and receive what you need monetarily, or demand that a partner soothe you in places that you did not even know were in pain.

Imagine a person who has never known that passionate love existed suddenly experiencing it in her life. Imagine someone who has lived her life paycheck to paycheck suddenly demanding and receiving abundance and generosity. This is not only a gift of crisis, but also a requirement of its resolution.

Whatever you need, right now, in this moment of crisis, is what you will have forever after in your life.

Finding the Home You May Never Have Had

When we were children, home was where our grown-ups were. They defined our world. It did not matter whether it was a good home or a difficult one — it was where we belonged, where we were connected to life.

As we grew a little older, the boundaries of home grew along with us. Home was now defined by the house in which we lived, our friends, our school, our town, our country, and as we matured even more, by our beliefs and allegiances.

As adults we create our literal homes. We have the capacity to choose, to some degree, where we live, with whom we relate, and what we believe in. Home, however, has a greater sense. Home is the place we belong and where we thrive — physically, spiritually, mentally, socially, and energetically. Home is the place we go to recharge and nourish from the difficult task of being in human bodies and dealing with the inconsistencies of life. In the world, in the energetic oneness of the universe, and in ourselves, home is where we belong. There is always a safe place for us at home.

Many of us have not been home in a very long time. By the time we reach maturity, we have too much information in the form of internal patterns and programming acquired from the experiences and expectations of our upbringing, our peer groups, our experiences in the world, and the overwhelming expectations of our popular culture. It is our task to grow beyond these patterns, to find the person within ourselves that we choose to be and then to create the life that we choose to live; to create our true home.

Life is full of surprising twists. The unexpected and unprepared for are the things that we should anticipate. This is how the universe helps us grow. The only real certitude in life is the ability to respond to change: a nourishing elixir of inner resources and outer support that we are trained in as children or that we acquire as adults. Even for the child gifted with this elixir, traumatic changes can overwhelm her ability to cope. A crisis requires her to reach beyond what she knows to heal.

Resilience is an essential gift to have in a successful life. It is the ability to find your way home and to re-create home for yourself, from anywhere, within any experience in life. This book is about resilience. Each chapter has been created to take you, one step at a time, closer to home, to the place you want and need to be. In order to do this for all of my readers, I have assumed the worst state: the state of crisis, when all of your home structures have been assaulted by life. Learning these steps, even if you are not in crisis, will help you create your life consciously each day.

We all know people who have been the victims of their destiny and those, on the contrary, who re-create themselves in the image of their dreams. Wherever you are right now in your life, you can choose where you go next. Home is the place where you find the intuition, inspiration, and resources to be your dreams and not your destiny.

Exercise: Finding and Following Your Inner Wisdom

By this point in the book, you have probably noticed that there exists a wise you, a reactive you, and a critical you. Of course the reactive, instinctive you is the one that rises up habitually in any situation. To move from crisis to a new life, you need truly to know and communicate with the wise you. Only then will you trust her enough to guide your life.

Once again, keeping a notebook will show you proof positive that you can be trusted as a source of inspiration, information, and help. The mind is a messy place; having things in black and white helps you use them more effectively.

This is a simple exercise. You'll need your journal or a notebook; you can use a tape recorder if you prefer. First, consider the following question:

If anyone could guide you, answer your questions about the past, the present, and the future, help you understand your gifts, what would you ask that person?

Record your responses. When you have done so, get up, walk around a bit, and then sit down in a place where there is space in front of you for this special person.

Now imagine your wise, all-knowing self in that space before you. You know everything that you need to know, and you know how to change what you need to change about your present and your future. Ask yourself the questions you recorded, one by one.

Take time to say the answer as you hear it or know it.

You will know when you are speaking from your wisdom and when you are not. The answer won't sound right to you or will make you anxious or angry or depressed or avoidant — depending on your type.

Let yourself go on and on. Often you will start from what your "daily" self thinks or hopes or fears and as you speak, you will get to the truth. Remember, your wise self can help you change things in your life, so if you hear something difficult, ask your wise self how you can change it or prepare yourself in a way that can make even difficult moments successful and meaningful.

Return to this exercise from time to time. You will get more out of the exercise the more times you complete it.

SHARING THE BLESSINGS

The Power of Usefulness

Twenty years ago I worked with a man, Mr. B, who was in the last days of liver cancer at a public hospital. He was uneducated, poor, and clearly in the process of dying. Mr. B had grown up in an extended family in the Deep South.

I visited him daily to do laying on of hands to decrease his pain. Every morning when I arrived at his bed, there was a veritable salon of other patients hanging out in his room, chatting. He was listening, dispensing advice, a pat on the hand, giving all the warmth that he had grown up with back to these patients, some of whom had no one else to talk to.

He died giving. I am not even sure that he had lived that way. He was an alcoholic and had battled poverty his whole life. In the end he left many people feeling peaceful in a traumatic environment.

৯৹

You always have something of great value to give. What you have to give may change as you change. Some people will be uncomfortable with the change. Some will feel blessed by it. You will draw new people to you with your new gifts. You may not even know what you are giving.

The act of being useful is a powerful survival cue for the subconscious. We see that older people who remain useful remain viable — physically, emotionally, and economically. When you are helping others through crisis — especially children — it is important to acknowledge in what ways they are still useful and valuable in your life and in the world.

Although children have the right to be loved and supported by virtue of their childhood, the single most empowering thing we can do to help our children — or
anyone for that matter — handle crises well is to affirm
for them the many ways in which they are useful to others.
This step can be something as simple as acknowledging
their citizenship when they pick up litter from the street,
to encouraging them to use their understanding to include
a child who is not popular. Although most children have
chores, many have no idea how much they assist us by
completing those chores. A simple, "Thank you for putting the dishes away. It gave me the time to play this game
with you and enjoy myself," is good training for resilience.
When generosity is the rule, isolation — the number-one
danger of crisis — is rare.

When Others Are in Crisis: What to Do
When Your Loved Ones Hurt

When someone we love is in crisis, we are affected in a variety of ways. Many marriages end because one partner is in crisis and the other falls into crisis as well. Families can unravel when a child is in crisis. Friendships end just when they are most needed when crisis is mismanaged by the personal community of friendship. There are more healing options when someone you love is going through change. It is important to know your type as well as theirs so you avoid the pitfalls of sharing crisis and focus on maintaining solid ground.

When a loved one is in crisis, there are two perspectives to manage. The person's crisis needs to be addressed as well as your reaction to it. This perspective is even harder to maintain when you appear to be the focus of the other person's crisis, such as in a marriage when your husband decides that he doesn't love you anymore or when your adolescent feels that you are ruining his life.

We feel most powerless when those we love are in pain or are harming themselves. We are part of their world, something that by the nature of crisis is undergoing change. Each person, however, is composed of himself and his world. You can be a part of someone else's healing while protecting yourself from the devastating effect of sharing crisis in a way that harms you. Take care of yourself first. Remember to take type into consideration.

ꝏ

Put on your own oxygen mask before helping others.

Every time we get on an airplane, my son and I have a running joke. When the flight attendant says, "In case of emergency, oxygen masks will fall from the compartment above you. Put on your own mask before helping others," we think to ourselves, "Yeah, right." We both know that I would always put on his mask first. I would be deluding myself to think otherwise.

Many years ago I had a student who was an emergency-room nurse. The AIDS epidemic had just begun. She was in crisis because she had neglected to put on gloves during a particularly busy moment at work, and she had gotten a patient's blood on a cut on her hand. She was worried that she had become infected.

As a group we looked at her life. She had forgotten to put on her metaphoric "gloves" many times, allowing herself to be harmed to serve other people's more urgent needs. At the time, she was under the care of at least four doctors as a result of not caring for her health, both emotional and physical. She "got" that she didn't protect herself, so this was not news to her.

She was underwhelmed by our observations. "What if one of the patients had died because of the delay?" she argued. "Patients die all the time. How do you know that not taking ten seconds to protect yourself saved a patient?" "What if you were infected and had infected your patient?" countered another.

The bottom line is that for your safety and the safety of everyone around you, you should "put on your own mask first, before helping others." You are your responsibility. If you don't take care of yourself, you cannot care for others. In fact, if you don't take care of yourself, you can burden and even endanger others.

My son is now thirteen. To my great relief I realize that he now knows how to put on his own mask.

ॐ

During crisis we need to be vigilant about injury. To help others in crisis, we need to make sure that there is enough support coming in to allow them to reorganize in a way that compensates for their loss. Often the only thing that we can do is provide support and, if they are open to it, help them structure the activities that are prescribed for their type. When you provide type-appropriate structure for someone in crisis, you give that person a "world" to bridge the gap between her old life and her new one.

ॐ

People in crisis are often victimized by others. Fending off the crisis, they are scarcely able to defend themselves from further attack. Ironically, people close to "the victim" will often use the person's crisis as an opportunity to vent long-held resentments or vendettas. As mammals, we are genetically programmed to prey on those weaker, or we would have been eaten early on. There is a more enlightened choice. We can notice when others around us are in crisis and take it upon ourselves to provide protection in a variety of empowering ways.

- Relate to the person and not the crisis. This may mean making rules like putting the person on a crisis "talk diet" (for example, limit any discussion of the crisis to no more than three minutes of any conversation).
- Reaffirm the person's positive and functional qualities.
- Affirm that the person's truth lies within.
- Offer loyalty and protection in his or her environment.
- Choose to act with kindness even when the person is maddening (as people in crisis often are).
- Point out alternate behaviors and ways of expression that would help him or her be less maddening.
- Hold the belief and vision that the person is powerful and complete, despite the current flux.
- Be inclusive. Invite and encourage the person to be a functional part of your community.

- Require behaviors that force the person to function effectively, such as joining a group of friends for dinner or working out in the gym.
- Know when you are near your tolerance limit and take a break. Set boundaries. Do not allow yourself to be drained.

When someone drops to the bottom of the food chain, you bring out your inner healer when you support that person. In doing so you transform yourself in ways that will bring you immeasurable joy in your life.

Response Types Are Communicable

Living with someone who is anxious can put you in a state of constant agitation. Beware of absorbing the anxiety, getting hostile, or inappropriately distancing from the person or situation.

Living with someone who is rageful can erode your sense of self. Beware of placating in a way in which you lose yourself and erode your own sense of control and self-determination.

Living with someone in denial can be exhausting. Beware of taking the lion's share of the burden as your own, as you may feel that you have to be continually in touch with the difficult aspects of life's realities for two.

Living with someone who is depressed can be depressing. Beware of feeling overly responsible, powerless to create change, and then, ultimately, angry.

৵

When you are trying to help an anxiety type, you need to know that this person cannot be reassured by your words. He or she cannot feel safety. The way to help someone in anxiety is to ground his confusion in compelling and useful tasks that can have some sense of completion. He has to be doing things that feel empowering and create good results. He needs to be guided to activities that focus his energy. He needs to be engaged in a way that allows him to push away his unprofitable ruminations that threaten to consume him. Do not engage in his ruminating, "what if, what do you think, what should I do" inner dialog with him. Anxiety types need the awareness that if they stop fretting, everything around them will not disintegrate.

๛

When you are trying to help anger types, you need to give them some initial space to discharge their anger. They are incapable of letting you in without harming you when they are at their most explosive. When they cause harm, they feel shame, which fuels the anger.

At an appropriate, low-intensity time, you need to guide anger types to more appropriate discharge outlets (outlined in prescriptions for anger). Once they master the feelings of the moment, your next step is to encourage them to employ denial and get them to focus on what they want to create. Help them to step away from passion and to evaluate their situation when their head is cool.

Do not engage in battle with an anger type, support an enraged point of view, or play the devil's advocate. Anger types need the awareness that they can never be made whole through another person's pain.

๛

When you are trying to help denial types, take them to movies that evoke emotion. Show them an album of pictures that evoke feeling. Give them a favorite childhood book and read it to them. Engage in activities that allow them to feel without being overwhelmed by feeling. It is rarely helpful to throw reality in their faces. You can, however, structure situations where it is safe for them to feel and acknowledge their own awareness, often through shared activity. I am sure that the concept of parallel play was coined by a denial type. Two people playing side by side but not together. Be available but not intrusive. Do not, however, be maneuvered into participating in their denial stories. With denial types who are insisting that you share the fantasy, silence is a virtue. Denial types need to know that they can see and feel without being overwhelmed.

෫ੇ

When you are trying to help a depression type, support normal daily activities. Run the shower, serve the breakfast, bring the phone, help the person fight the draw to inaction by supporting action, making it easier. Depression types need to feel that they have the strength to engage in the pulse of life.

❧

When you are helping someone in crisis, you need to recognize when his or her crisis or the stress of taking your focus off your own need has put you in your danger zone: you find yourself falling back into old thoughts, feelings or behaviors, or you begin getting sloppy about taking care of "earth reality," the necessary yet mundane, everyday tasks that keep your life on course. Remember, crisis is a communicable disease. If you are not taking care of yourself while supporting the other person, you will disintegrate into the pathology of *your* type. When you begin to experience any of your type's typical symptoms, follow the prescriptions we discussed earlier. Snatch moments of transcendence; make a deposit to your emotional currency account.

If you notice other people in your group falling into to these danger zones, encourage them to do the same. The unity engendered through moving through crisis together in a healing, productive way is among the strongest bonds you can create in a family or a group. The assurance that each person at his or her worst can still function from love, wholeness, and integrity connects you to one another in a place of infinite, intrinsic depth. You affirm that even when you are hurt, you will not harm, and when another is hurting, you will respond without judgment.

Some of the strongest friendships, families, and companies are created and strengthened through times of crisis. To remain true to this responsibility, be aware of your danger zone and the danger zone of those around you.

⁓

If you are an anxiety type, you know that you are in your danger zone when you cannot get beyond your worries to do something constructive for yourself. You become immersed in minutiae and in fears that have nothing to do with the present moment. Avoid old, safe worries that are self-perpetuating. Your imagination can take you to disastrous outcomes of supreme proportions.

⁓

If you are a denial type, you know that you are in your danger zone when inside you feel that you are doing well but outside you are standing in an earthquake: when the people you care about around you are not doing well or when people around you are concerned about you, and you don't understand why or respond. You will find yourself being overcritical to those who matter instead of coping with the crisis at hand. Your imagination has deserted you entirely.

If you are depressed you know you are in the danger zone when you can't imagine having the energy to finish this book. Nothing seems worth the effort: body maintenance, gym, even showers have become too much to handle. You don't see any way out of your situation. You feel that this is your permanent condition. You don't foresee that anything will ever change. Your imagination takes you to how happy everyone else is and how unhappy you will always remain.

If you are an anger type, you know that you are in your danger zone when you begin to feel resentful. You start measuring what you are doing against what is being done for you, and you keep coming up short. You have pushed down your needs, and now you feel them pushing back. Everyday occurrences begin to make you angry, and you feel like lashing out. You feel like nothing you are doing is enough, and that makes you mad.

Some Parting Words to the Different Types

Let me speak to denial types first, before you lose or "misplace" this book. Denial serves a purpose, and you hold on tight to your denial. If your denial is working for you, then you are not reading this book. Your life is working, right? If you are reading this book, denial is not doing its job. See anxiety. Denial types, if you are anxious, you are actually really doing something very brave and very right. You, of all people, can manage your life. Seeing what is wrong is only going to help you use your formidable skills to make a better life.

❧

Anxiety types, I know that you were getting frustrated waiting as I spoke to denial. The only positive thing that your disorganizing anxiety is doing is perhaps helping you burn more calories. You are probably making your situation worse by taking compulsive action while freezing when you have to marshal real strength and resources. Mindless denial is your goal. When something makes you "forget" for a minute, do more of it. Just pretend it is all going to be okay. If you take your eye off the problem for a moment, you may see the solution, at which point you can harness your formidable energy to move the world.

Depression types, I know that you don't want to hear anything that is going to make you expend the energy to move from where you are now. However, things can't really get any worse. You may as well do the things that you were too afraid to do — demand support, reach out to people even if you are afraid they may reject you. If they do you will probably get angry; in fact the effort to move at all will make you angry, and anger will fuel necessary movement and action. You will be amazed at just how much energy anger provides. When you couple anger with your powerful and profound understanding of self, you can become anything you want and move into a life that supports who you really want to be.

జీ

Anger types, the only way that you can take power is by taking responsibility. Rage is the close cousin of remorse. You regret all that you have missed and all of the things that rage has ruined in your life. Pretend everything really is your fault, you really did mess up, you thought someone else's pain or remorse would make you whole, but it didn't. If you do this well, it will depress you. Depression will make your passion insightful, manageable, and ultimately constructive. You may not get back what you lost, but you will be able to build what is significant and valuable to you now. When you couple the self-awareness of depression with the passion of anger, you can build a life of your choosing that is rich in feeling, meaning, and self-actualization.

No Life Is Crisis Proof —
But Any Life Can Be
Less Crisis Prone

All change is an opportunity to open the possibilities of your life. We are creatures of habit.
Abused children put in a safe environment often
want to go back to their abusive parents. Even if a situation is less than ideal — and sometimes when it's awful —
we cling to it with an irrational intensity born of habit and
fear. When change or crisis allows us the opportunity to
become fully aware of our deepest needs and to realize
them in the world, we become vulnerable. So much of the
layered structure of our life and beliefs is challenged that

the essential, true needs of our being are exposed even if you cannot see them.

Adaptability can be an acquired skill, though some people are innately more adaptable than others. They seem always to build something better on the ashes of their past. Even so, there are some moments when a change or series of changes can temporarily overwhelm our ability to adapt, even for the most resilient individuals. When you feel like you are losing, you are in good company.

Although some of us are more resilient than others, different types are adaptive in different situations. Someone who bounces back when a financial crisis hits may not be as adaptable if the situation involves emotional abandonment. Depending on your childhood experiences, your personality, your external supports, your values, and even your genetics, you will find some kinds of crises easier to manage than others. You can, however, become generally more resilient by integrating certain patterns and behaviors into your life.

ૐ

The resilient individual:

- lives in the present
- values other people and reaches out when in need
- sees life as self-determined and forever challenging
- acts as if she has the tools to survive, even when she has her doubts
- acts as if she has much to give others and gives generously
- acts as if the world has enough for everyone, and demands from it accordingly
- has the courage to feel and love
- practices gratitude for self, for others, and for life
- has a good sense of her needs, limits, and boundaries

You can become more resilient by practicing these attributes even before you believe them. By practicing resilience you will repattern your attitudes and actions for positive change.

These attitudes can be taught. You can model them for your friends, spouse, parents, and children. How you view your circumstances profoundly affects your ability to survive dramatic change. Be vigilant about creating a good mythology of life in which you are the hero of your own story. If you live this truth, you create this truth.

Some people go through extreme personal upheavals and use their tribulations to excel, while other individuals are beaten down and defeated by life's crises. Why?

A study of adult victims of childhood abuse found that neither the degree nor the duration of the abuse predicted the degree of harm in their adult lives, but rather how much control the individual felt as a child he or she had in the process did. Those children who felt in greater control of what was going on — even if this sense of control was not objectively the case — tended to thrive as adults in spite of their abuse. This book has given you many tools to help you respond dynamically to crisis and change. These tools need to be integrated into your life and practiced so you can respond to future changes in a positive, joyful, and empowering way.

Conscious living can be an alternative to moving blindly from crisis to crisis. When you evolve, so do your opportunities — as does your capacity for joy and success. Working through crisis by working on self is empowering because your self is in your direct power to change. It is through evolving self that we either change our circumstances or use the power of locomotion to create a new environment.

Choose the Myths You Live By

Beware of embracing myths such as that you have only one life path, or one soul mate, or one chance for happiness or success, which of course you have lost and will never have again. Such myths are dangerous. Simple observation of life will show you conclusively that they are untrue. Second, third, fourth, fifth chances are abundant — for every human being, even you! You can move through your crisis in such a way that you create a life for yourself so intensely authentic and joyful that you could not, from your old perspective, have even dreamed it.

We have a rule in our house: *everything* is good luck. Broken mirror? Good luck. Step on a crack? Good luck. Lose your favorite necklace? It's making room for something better. You give the magic to your own myths. Be vigilant about creating good stories for yourself and for those you love.

You are creating your life right now, in this moment. There is no place for fear in a life consciously created by you. You now have the tools to deal with the feelings of loss created by change in your life. Nobody's life is immune from change. But each change, when guided by awareness, is an opportunity for a better life, and self — a better you — to emerge.

ACKNOWLEDGMENTS

This book began with my agent, Jennifer Rudolph Walsh. Jennifer, you have changed my life in so many ways. In the complete absence of appropriate words to convey all that I feel and owe, I must simply say thank you.

This book comes to you, the reader, thanks to the work of many talented people. Jennifer and I chose my publisher because of the great team they offered: Judy Clain, my editor, challenged me until this book became so much stronger than the original idea. The Heathers — Heather Rizzo and Heather Fain — and Sophie Cottrell, who had the press structured ten minutes after I handed in the final manuscript. Michael Pietsch, the publisher, who put them all together. Every time this book or I needed insight or support you went one step further than asked. I am fortunate to be at Little, Brown. Thank you. I also want to thank Rickie Harvey, the freelance copyeditor hired by Peggy Freudenthal, the copyediting manager at Little, Brown, for her fine-tuning of the manuscript. Please, promise me you will work on everything I do!

In a time of crisis there is no room for error or delay. I picked the brain of every psychiatrist and psychotherapist I know to make sure that the ideas herein would work for a diverse group of people. I would like to offer my special thanks to Leslie Klepper, the Brooklyn-based psychotherapist and director of a mental-health clinic where crisis is the daily special. Leslie went over all the tests in this book and every concept until they were perfect.

Everything built is created by many hands. I am blessed with a community of friends, clients, and family members. My readers have been so generous with their feedback and ideas about how to make my work more useful to them. Thank you for your support and for spreading the word. My private practice overflows. Thankfully, however, I have the privilege of training others. To my students, many of whom are now practitioners themselves, thank you for proving me a good teacher by surpassing me in both wisdom and skill.

My special thanks for this particular book go to Adam Robinson (my love), David Globus (Daddy), Sarah Globus (baby sister), and my mother, Vivian Globus (of blessed memory).

I love to see the names of my nieces and nephews all together; everything is now for you: Vivian and Ori Goldfield, Zach and Isabelle Rodriguez, Annie and Charlie Wallach, Gillian and Amanda Eisenberg, and Jake and Nicky Nathanson.

Samson Day, you are my own sun and light. It amazes me that you are now at an age to give your valuable insight and original support to all that I do. Who knew that life would get even better!

About the Author

LAURA DAY has been teaching individuals and companies to develop and apply intuitive solutions to their problems for over twenty years. She is the bestselling author of *Practical Intuition* and *The Circle*. Laura has been featured on *Oprah* and *The View* and many other national television shows as well as in other media. Laura's global clientele includes celebrities, scientists, business executives, and professionals in many fields. Laura trains facilitators across the country and holds free open training in New York City. She can be reached at www.practicalintuition.com.